Praying and
Teaching the Psalms

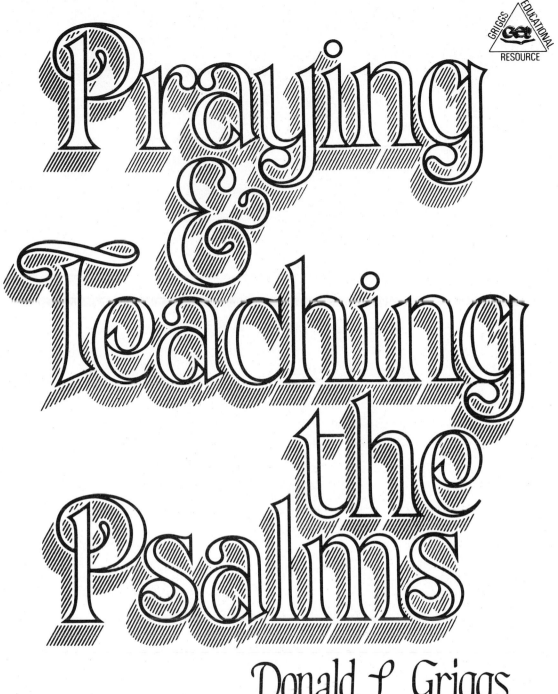

Praying & Teaching the Psalms

Donald L. Griggs

Illustrations by Becky Kehret

A Griggs Educational Resource
published by
ABINGDON PRESS / Nashville

PRAYING AND TEACHING THE PSALMS

Library of Congress Cataloging in Publication Data

Griggs, Donald L.
    Praying and teaching the Psalms.
    (A Griggs educational resource)
    Bibliography: p.
    Includes index.
      1. Bible. O.T. Psalms—Study. 2. Bible. O.T. Psalms—Prayers.
I. Title.
BS1430.5.G75   1984   223'.206   84-3108

ISBN 0-687-33633-3

MANUFACTURED BY THE PARTHENON PRESS AT
NASHVILLE, TENNESSEE, UNITED STATES OF AMERICA

Dedicated to
the faculty, staff, and students
of the
Presbyterian School of Christian Education
Richmond, Virginia,
a Graduate Center for Educational Ministry

Contents

Preface

Four years ago a group of students and I met in my living room for an hour each Wednesday night reading, discussing, meditating, and praying with the book of Psalms as our focus. Those weeks with the Psalms and my ten friends opened up a way of approaching the Psalms that was new for all of us. All of us were inspired by the realization that the words of the Psalmist addressed to God could be our words also.

My experiences with Psalms prompted me to volunteer to teach an adult Bible class at the Second Presbyterian Church in Richmond, Virginia. With another group of highly motivated folks, I spent ten weeks working with the Psalms in a more formal, structured way. Those original session plans have been revised, tested, and revised again for a number of groups. Three particular groups provided a lot of helpful feedback as they participated enthusiastically in the study of Psalms. A class of the Laity School in the fall of 1981 and a continuing education group in the spring of 1982 at the Presbyterian School of Christian Education, in Richmond, Virginia, provided the occasion for spending significant amounts of time exploring the Psalms in some depth. Most recently I spent five days with a group of pastors and lay persons at a conference of the Synod of the Pacific, Presbyterian Church (USA), at Asilomar, California, where we worked with parts of the first draft of this book. I am greatly indebted to all the pastors, educators, students, and church members with whom I have had the pleasure to explore the Psalms. Each person will know that he or she is remembered here, and many will recognize parts of the book they experienced in a more rudimentary form.

Time for writing *Praying and Teaching the Psalms* was provided by a leave of absence from my work at the Presbyterian School of Christian Education made possible by President Heath Rada and Dean Charles Melchert. Associations with my faculty colleagues, the students in the graduate programs, and participants in continuing education events—on and off campus—have been a continual source of nurture, encouragement, and critique. Though I assume full responsibility for all that I have written, I could not have done it without the interaction with these many companions who have shared the journey with me.

As with all my writing projects the words of my pen would never see the printer's ink without the significant contributions of my partner, friend, and wife, Pat. Pat not only typed the first and second drafts, she also served as editor, designer, critic, and advocate. Pat worked long hours on a house-refurbishing project during our leave of absence to allow me the time to read and think and write. The reader will not notice all of the places where her questions and comments influenced the shape of the final product, but Pat and I will recognize them.

Two other words of appreciation must be expressed. Becky Kehret of San Leandro, California, a student at the Academy of Arts in San Francisco, has been a special friend since she was a toddler. Becky brings a youthful, fresh interpretation to the Psalms with her drawings. I appreciate very much Becky's creativity and am pleased to introduce her to you. I must also express my appreciation to the American Bible Society for their willingness to allow me to use so much from the *Good News Bible* in the Today's English Version. You will notice throughout the book why I am so appreciative of that particular translation.

It has been an inspiring four years and an especially significant summer spent with the Psalms. I believe that my personal spiritual development has been profoundly enhanced by the Psalms. I feel that my work as a teacher and pastor for years to come will show the effect of my having spent so much time with the Psalms. And, I am quite confident I will be spending many, many more hours with Psalms as they continue to speak to me of God's amazing grace and as they enable me to express my own feelings and beliefs to God.

Donald L. Griggs
Livermore, California, and
Richmond, Virginia
Summer 1983

Introduction

When I first planned to write this book, I thought I would need a much longer introduction to provide a lot of information about Psalms. However, it has been more effective to include as much background information as possible in the context of the specific praying and teaching activities. All of the information about Psalms that I wanted to share with the reader has been presented throughout the twenty chapters.

In working with the Psalms to develop the twenty praying and teaching activities, I have come to appreciate the value and the richness of the Psalms as holy scripture. The Psalms are the word of God for our day in the sense that God speaks to us about who God is, who the human person is, and what their relationship is to each other. The Psalms are also the words of a Psalmist who speaks directly to God of the faith and fear, the praise and lament, and the trust and doubt that the people of God experience. The words of Psalms were conceived in a particular time and place in response to real-life and faith experiences. These words arise from experiences with which we can all identify, evoking in us thoughts and emotions that may or may not be similar to their origins but nevertheless are as real and genuine for us as the words were for the Psalmist. The words of the Psalms have a life of their own. We read the words in order to search for their original meaning as well as read them for their vivid expression of what the contemporary believer thinks and feels at the moment. The Psalms can be read and reread, and their meanings will never be exhausted. New meanings, new truths, new experiences of God will emerge with each reading for a whole lifetime. That is the nature of holy scripture, and it is especially true of the Psalms.

Whereas many of the Psalms have become meaningful and memorable for me, there is a portion of one Psalm that seems to set the stage for all the Psalms and especially for my own approach to the Psalms. Psalm 78:1-7 is an introduction to a lengthy salvation history Psalm. That same passage serves as an introduction to the purpose and approach of this book.

Listen, my people, to my teaching,
  and pay attention to what I say.
I am going to use wise sayings
  and explain mysteries from the past,
  things we have heard and known,
  things that our [parents] told us.
We will not keep them from our children;
  we will tell the next generation
  about the Lord's power and his great deeds
  and the wonderful things he has done.

He gave laws to the people of Israel
  and commandments to the descendants of
    Jacob.
He instructed our ancestors
  to teach his laws to their children,
so that the next generation might learn them
  and in turn should tell their children.
In this way they also would put their trust in
    God
  and not forget what he has done,
  but always obey his commandments.
                                Psalm 78:1-7

This is the perfect passage to read for a teacher dedication or recognition service. The teachers in our churches are very much a part of the tradition of which the passage speaks—where one generation is responsible for telling The Story of their faith to the next generation so that they in turn will be able to tell The Story to their children. That is exactly what the teachers in the church are doing, and it is to that storytelling task that I am committed.

We could develop an educational theory based upon Psalm 78:1-7. Within those few verses there are clues for the purpose of teaching, the content of teaching, and the expectations of those who are taught. The *purpose* of the teaching is to explain "mysteries from the past" so that those who hear the explanation may be able to "put their trust in God." That is also the purpose of this book, to try to explain some of the mysteries of the Psalms and of the faith and life to which the Psalms attest. I hope you, the readers, will experience the opening of many windows of insight as you read the Psalms, guided by the resources of this book. If that happens to some degree, then there will be many others in the groups and classes led by you who will also have many mysteries explained to them.

The *content* or the curriculum of the teaching included wise sayings, the Lord's great deeds, and the laws and commandments. That is basically the content of the Psalms and all of scripture. Wise sayings, or parables as translated by the Revised Standard Version are those truths that are essential to knowing who God is and who the human is in relation to God. This truth is presented in such a way that every person desiring to know who God is is capable of understanding that truth. The Lord's great deeds are too numerous to count. Many of those actions are recorded in scripture; many more are recorded in the annals of sacred history; and many more are experienced by God's people even today. The laws and commandments are presented in the Pentateuch and were part of the Psalmist's treasured heritage. Many of those laws and commandments continue to be relevant for the modern person. For we Christians, who are guided by the words of Jesus, all the laws and commandments are summarized by his two great commandments: love God with your whole being and love your neighbor as yourself. In many ways the three aspects of the content of the teaching identified by Psalm 78:1-7 will be three important emphases of this book.

The passage also suggests explicitly what are the *expectations* included in the text. The hearers or learners are expected to:

1. listen (to the teachings)
2. tell others (about the Lord's power and great deeds)
3. teach (the next generation)
4. trust (God)
5. remember (what God has done)
6. obey (God's commandments)

Those are worthy objectives for the teacher and worthy responses by the learners. We engage in an important enterprise as we prepare to teach others in the groups and classes of our churches. This book is committed to fulfilling these objectives.

It was difficult deciding whether the first chapters should focus on teaching activities or on praying activities. Could it be that if persons were introduced to Psalms through teaching activities they would be better equipped to participate in praying activities? Or should praying activities set the stage for learning more about Psalms in teaching activities? I have opted for the latter because of the nature of the Psalms; they are first and foremost prayers and hymns. The Psalms are essentially devotional literature and should be approached first through the disciplines of the spiritual life. If we never spent a single moment in a teaching-learning session with the Psalms, it would still be important to experience the Psalms in prayer and worship. Thus, I have outlined ten praying activities followed by ten teaching activities.

All of the praying and teaching activities are designed to enable maximum participation by the members of the groups or classes with which they are shared. There are several features of the praying and teaching activities that should be understood by the leaders/teachers who use them.

1. In each chapter, there is a "Setting the Stage" section. This section is important for understanding the intent, the format, and some of the content of each activity.
2. There are no designations for the amount of time necessary for each part of each activity. Occasionally I give clues regarding amounts of time, but it will be necessary for the teacher/leader to plan carefully so that the amount of time available will match as closely as possible the amount of time necessary for the parts of the planned activity. Flexibility is important. Activities as they are outlined suggest what is possible. Leaders/teachers are responsible for adapting and adjusting these suggestions for their own situations.
3. Each praying and teaching activity includes a series of directions or suggestions. Sometimes the directions are listed clearly in a step-one, step-two, step-three format, and other times the directions are embodied in a series of paragraphs. Either way, the directions should be explicit and complete enough to enable most persons to be successful in accomplishing what was intended. Sometimes, the directions are

written specifically for the participants, other times for the teacher/leader.

4. The activities for the most part are inductive. Even in chapters 11 and 12 where a large amount of content is presented, there are a few suggestions for involving participants in an inductive process. The emphasis is on process with the conviction that when the participants become involved in and responsible for the process, there is not only a greater potential for learning but also a much greater chance that the subject experienced will make a significant impact on the faith and life experiences of the person.

5. Even though there is a heavy emphasis on process and an inductive approach to praying and studying the Psalms, the leader/teacher should not hesitate to present information in a deductive, cognitive way when that may be the most efficient and appropriate way to deal with the material. The important thing is to keep a balance between the inductive and deductive approaches.

6. Even though the book is divided into two distinct parts, praying activities and teaching activities, the sections are not exclusively one or the other. In several of the praying activities, some information must be presented before the activitity can be experienced effectively. In most of the teaching activities there are opportunities for praying. Teachers/leaders will be most effective when they include elements of both praying and teaching in whichever activity they share with the participants.

Now, I would like to suggest a few ways that this book may be used. I can imagine some persons reading the book cover to cover for their own nurture and personal satisfaction. I hope that individuals who read this book as a resource for their own study will find challenges to their thinking and promptings of their spirits.

The nature of adult education in many churches where there are short-term elective courses suggests that this book may be used as a basis for devising session plans for as few as six and as many as thirteen or fifteen sessions. The book also may be a helpful resource to teachers who want some practical guidelines to augment their own thinking, planning, and creating as they work with a group in studying the Psalms.

A combination of praying and teaching activities can provide an excellent format for a weekend retreat or summer conference. The extended time available in retreat and conference settings allows for the kind of integration of studying, reflecting, praying, and creating that is proposed by the book's activities.

There are many times when groups and organizations desire to begin their meetings with brief periods of worship and/or study. The ten praying activities especially, but also parts of some of the teaching activities, would be very appropriate for fifteen to thirty minutes at the beginning of a meeting.

It is even possible that those teaching a course of study on the Psalms in a seminary or church college will find this book a helpful resource as both professors and students seek ways to share with others the great treasures of learnings about the Psalms that they experience in their studies.

This is not a scholarly book with a lot of footnotes. I read a lot of books and made a lot of notes. I am greatly indebted to many biblical scholars for their significant work. However, I have attempted to gather ideas from many of the sources, to summarize complex concepts and issues, and to use what is more in the realm of common knowledge rather than to get caught up in debating the fine points. The bibliography includes books and authors that have been most helpful to me. This is not an exhaustive bibliography on Psalms but a selective one. I trust that the readers will find the resources that are included in the bibliography to be representative of many points of view and to be of help.

Some final, brief notes must be presented before I can conclude this introduction and go to the heart of the book. There are some special concerns that I have had in mind throughout my writing and ways I have dealt with them intentionally. I have referred to those who guide others in groups or classes as teachers/leaders or as leaders/teachers. In many ways a person who guides others is both a leader and a teacher so rather than opting for one or the other I have combined them and alternated the way they appear. Those who experience these praying and teaching activities are usually identified as participants, members of a group, individuals, or persons so as to avoid the assumption that they are all students.

I write often of "the Psalmist." I do not have a particular author in mind as I use that designation. Rather I have in mind an individual or even a tradition, which can be personalized more by referring to the Psalmist instead of the author. Also, for better or worse, I have cast the Psalmist in the masculine gender.

Regarding gender, I have tried to avoid presenting God as masculine. Some of the sentences end up a little awkward, but in the end I am much more pleased to conceive of God without gender or to conceive of God in a more complete way, as representing both feminine and masculine. Where I have made third-person singular references, I have chosen not to use he/she but rather to alternate the personal pronoun so that in one sentence the references may be to "her" and in the next sentence "him."

Enough of the preliminaries—let's get involved with the praying and teaching activities that follow. It will be most helpful to read the chapters in sequence and then after gaining a sense of the whole, concentrate on one or more specific chapters.

PART ONE
Praying the Psalms: Ten Activities

Introduction

Some years ago I received my first copy of the Psalms translated by the American Bible Society in the Today's English Version (TEV). Even though I had read, studied, and memorized Psalms over the years, my reading in the TEV was the first time I became fully aware that the words were not just words of ancient, anonymous authors—they could also be my words. As I reflect on the experience, I realize that the contemporary, simple language of the TEV makes it more possible for me to identify personally with the concepts, images, and experiences expressed by the Psalmist. In the TEV the Psalms are translated in an informal language. God is addressed as "you" (instead of "thee" or "thou"), which is the way I speak to God in my own prayers. Also, the TEV translation makes it quite clear when the first-person singular is intended. As an example, of which there are a multitude, compare Psalm 30:11-12 in both RSV and TEV translations:

Revised Standard Version

Thou hast turned my mourning
   into dancing;
  thou hast loosed my sackcloth
  and girded me with gladness,
that my soul may praise thee
   and not be silent.
  O Lord my God, I will give
   thanks to thee for ever.

Today's English Version

You have changed my sadness
   into a joyful dance;
  you have taken away my sorrow
  and surrounded me with joy.
So I will not be silent;
  I will sing praise to you.
Lord, you are my God;
  I will give you thanks forever.

The RSV translation is beautiful with its classical form and style. If it were just a matter of studying and appreciating great literature, I might prefer the RSV translation. However, because the words of the Psalmist become the living word of God for me and provide the means for my speaking to and about God, the TEV provides the vehicle that will help me the most.

Many Psalms are written in the form of prayers. They are words addressed to God in praise, thanksgiving, confession, lament, and supplication. By my count at least seventy-four Psalms can be identified as prayers, which means that virtually half of the Psalms are written in this form. Of course, the Psalms are written from a personal and community life situation that is quite different from the world in which we live. The genius and divine inspiration of the Psalms are that the concerns, emotions, and experiences expressed therein transcend particular historical settings, community concerns, or individual experiences. The Psalms represent universal human experiences from the deepest despair to the highest exaltation. When the Psalmist cries, "My God, my God, why have you abandoned me?" (22:1), it is not a cry limited to one person in a particular time and place—it is also a cry voiced by Jesus as he suffers on the cross as well as a cry of parents today who grieve the death of their child. And when the Psalmist speaks, "O God, you are my God, and I long for you. My whole being desires you; like a dry, worn-out, and waterless land, my soul is thirsty for you" (63:1), it is not just the plea of a person from antiquity but it is also my plea as I speak to God of my own need of his presence in my life.

With this growing awareness that the prayers of the Psalmist could be prayers of God's people today, I have discovered that there are many ways individuals for themselves, as well as pastors and educators guiding others, can use the Psalms to enhance their experiences of praying. What follows is a series of ten activities that can be experienced by individuals as well as groups. Some of the activities will be as brief as five minutes, while other activities may take as long as a half hour. The activities were mostly designed for and used as the opening devotions for meetings, workshops, class sessions, or other group gatherings. Many of the activities can be adapted for inclusion in corporate worship, especially in midweek services, retreats or conferences, intergenerational worship, and/or smaller, informal Sunday worship services.

In reviewing these ten activities, it is important to consider several factors when determining how to implement an activity with a group.

1. *How much time do you have?*
   None of the activities should be rushed nor should shortcuts be used. After an experience of prayer using one of the activities, a participant reflecting on the experience said, "How could thirty minutes ever be too long to spend in prayer at the beginning of such an important meeting as this?"

2. *What is the nature of the group or event or what is the theme of the class or service?*
   It is important to match the approach to the Psalms or the theme of the Psalms to the group involved.

3. *What resources and equipment are needed?*
   If everyone needs the same translation of the Psalms, then copies of the Bible should be available for those who do not bring their own or do not have a copy of the translation being used. There may be other resources needed such as paper, pencils, hymnals, printed directions of an activity, filmstrip projector, cassette recorder, etc.

4. *How should the space be arranged?*
   For some activities and in some settings, it will not matter how the space is arranged. However, it may enhance the participant's involvement if the chairs are arranged in a circle or several rows in a semicircle. Gathering in the chapel, in the chancel of the sanctuary, or some other special place may be most appropriate.

1

Praying with the Psalmist

Setting the Stage

This activity requires the leader to select five to eight Psalm passages in advance. The passages could reflect a common theme, or they could be diverse. The passages need to be written on a sheet of newsprint, chalkboard, or transparency, or they could be duplicated on sheets of paper so that each person has a copy. It is important to identify each passage with a brief excerpt from the Psalm so that the participants will have some basis on which to make a choice. The directions could be given verbally, one step at a time after participants have completed each step. Give the following directions in your own words.

Select a Psalm

Select one of the following Psalm passages that you feel most comfortable with. Allow enough time for the participants to reflect on and respond to the passage.

(Sample passages)

1. Psalm 8:1-7	"What is man, that you think of him?"
2. Psalm 16:1-11	"I am always aware of the Lord's presence."
3. Psalm 25:1-14	"Keep your promise, Lord, and forgive my sins."
4. Psalm 30:1-12	"Lord . . . I will give you thanks forever."
5. Psalm 103:1-14	"Praise the Lord, my soul!"
6. Psalm 139:1-12	"Lord, you have examined me and you know me."

Read the Psalm

Read the selected passages to yourself. Read the words as if they were the words of your own prayer. Whenever you read "I," "my," "me," etc., read it as if that meant *you.*

Where could I go to escape from you?
  Where could I get away from your presence?
If I went up to heaven, you would be there;
  if I lay down in the world of the dead, you would be there.
If I flew away beyond the east
  or lived in the farthest place in the west,
You would be there to lead me,
  you would be there to help me.

Psalm 139:7-10

Add Personal Words to a Psalm Portion

From the passage you have read, select a phrase, a verse or two verses to be the words you will use to begin your own prayer. Write those words down and then continue writing an additional sentence or two of your own continuing the thoughts and feelings begun by the words of the Psalmist.

Share Psalm Prayers

Let us now spend a few minutes in prayer sharing the words of the Psalmist we selected and the words of prayer we have written. Individuals read their prayers aloud as they feel motivated to share.

Reflecting on the Process

The key element of this activity is that individuals are prompted by the words of the Psalms to pray. When they focus on a key Psalm passage, they are able to continue the thoughts of the Psalmist in their own words. It is sufficient for individuls to do the activity by and for themselves. However, there is an added benefit to a group's prayer experience when group members share with one another their prayers so that personal prayers become corporate prayers. In this activity it becomes very clear that individuals and a group are praying with the Psalmist as well as with each other.

It is important that sharing be an option. I avoid the custom of going around the circle, preferring to allow persons to participate, or not, as they choose. Sometimes I will begin the sharing, other times I will conclude it, and still other times I may not share my prayer at all. I always end the time of prayer with a loud deliberate "AMEN!" And, I may also invite the participants to respond with "Amen" by saying, "Let all the people say . . . AMEN!"

2

Psalms for Personal Meditation

Setting the Stage

Personal meditation can be experienced by oneself or with others in a group guided by a leader. If experienced by oneself, each of the following Psalms can serve as a basis for meditation at different times. The same process can be applied to other Psalms that an individual would select for personal meditation.

In a group the leader could use the following directions to guide individuals in the experience of meditation. The leader must be sensitive to the individuals in the group and aware that persons move at different rates. Some individuals may feel rushed; others may feel that the meditation is moving too slowly. The leader can alert the group to this reality and encourage members to be patient. By sensing how people are moving with the process and by being open to feedback, the leader will be able to adjust the pace of the process on other occasions when this same activity is used with the group.

The Leader May Give the Following Guidance to the Experience

Take ten to fifteen minutes individually to read and meditate upon one of the following Psalm passages. Brief directions will be given to guide the meditation. If you feel rushed, be patient, move at your own pace, skip a step in the process if you want to. If you feel that the process is moving too slowly, again be patient, repeat a step, or move to another Psalm and repeat the step.

The intent of this prayer activity of meditation is to lead you to be still, to focus on the words of the Psalm, to be open to God speaking to you in the quietness of this moment, and to respond with your own feeling, thinking, and speaking.

Select a Psalm Passage

Select one of the following Psalm passages. You may want to select a familiar one in order to receive new insights and blessings from that passage. Or you may prefer to select an unfamiliar passage, so that you may approach it from a fresh perspective and be open to receive the surprises contained therein. Be willing to spend the next ten to fifteen minutes meditating upon the Psalm of your choice.

Select One Passage

1. Psalm 11:1-7   "I trust in the Lord for safety."
2. Psalm 16:1-11   "You, Lord, are all I have."
3. Psalm 23:1-6   "The Lord is my shepherd."

20

4. Psalm 32:1-11   "Happy are those whose sins are forgiven."

5. Psalm 62:1-12   "[God] alone protects and saves me."

6. Psalm 63:1-8   "O God . . . My whole being desires you."

7. Psalm 86:1-13*a*   "Teach me, Lord, what you want me to do."

8. Psalm 121:1-8   "My help will come from the Lord."

Read the Selected Passage

Read the passage you selected in quiet and privacy. Read every word, pausing when necessary in order to let each word present itself to you. Read the words as if you had never read or heard them before. Be open to new insights that may come.

Meditate upon the Passage

After participants have read their passages carefully, the leader can ask one, two, or more of the following questions. After asking each question, provide a minimum of one minute of silence to allow time for meditation.

1. What one word, phrase, or verse speaks most loudly to you? Read that portion of the passage again and again.

2. What experience of the Psalmist seems to be most distant from your experience? Why?

3. What experience of the Psalmist do you identify with most closely? Why?

4. What feelings are expressed by the Psalmist? How do these feelings compare with

My soul will feast and be satisfied,
and I will sing glad songs of praise to you.
Psalm 63:5

feelings you have had in your relationship with God?

5. If you were to add your own words to the words of the Psalmist, what would those words be?

Read Your Partner's Passage

There should be three or four minutes remaining for the last step of the process. Except for spoken directions by the leader, most of the time to this point has been in silence. In this last step there will be much chatter as each individual hears her Psalm read by a partner.

Each individual teams up with a partner. If one person is left over, that person and the leader may be partners. In this part of the process, one person reads the Psalm passage chosen by his partner.

When reading to their partners, each individual may preface the reading of the Psalm passage by addressing their partner with the words, "(name of person), hear God's word through the Psalmist for you." After one member of the pair has read to his partner, then the other partner should read to the other. When the leader observes that all the pairs have completed their readings, she says "AMEN! Let all the people say . . . 'AMEN!' "

Reflecting on the Process

As in the first activity, Psalm passages provide the basis for individual prayers and meditation. The activity could be completed following the meditation on the Psalm guided by the key questions. However, there is a dynamic present in hearing the Psalm read to oneself by another that is missing when one just reads and meditates alone in silence. There is even an additional bonus when a number of persons are reading all at the same time . The leader need not worry that several, a dozen or more persons all reading aloud simultaneously, will disturb those listening. Individuals are able to filter out all the other readers in order to concentrate on the words their partners are reading.

3

Prayers of Praise

Setting the Stage

Participants can accomplish the two primary tasks of this activity in five to ten minutes. Because of the nature of the activity, it could be repeated a number of times in the course of a group's life together. The same directions could be used along with changing the theme, so that the focus of the prayers becomes something new. It is necessary for each participant to have a personal copy of the Bible. The Bibles can be the same translation or different translations. I have found the Bible in Today's English Version to be especially helpful because of the descriptive headings that are included with each Psalm. The headings in boldface type also assist individuals in the process of skimming.

Leading the Activity

For the next few minutes, we want to focus on Psalms of praise. There are many Psalms that are primarily hymns of praise, and there are many other Psalms with isolated verses expressing the theme of praise to God. Take about four or five minutes to skim a number of Psalms. Start any place you want. Look at the headings in the margins or at the beginning of each Psalm. Skim

Sing for joy to the Lord, all the earth;
praise him with songs and shouts of joy!

Psalm 98:4

quickly, seeking to identify several Psalms of praise. When you locate such a Psalm or brief passage, read it quickly. As you read several passages, try to select one to three verses of praise to God that express your own feelings and thoughts. Focus on these few verses by reading them prayerfully again and again. Be prepared to share your prayer of praise, using the Psalm verses you selected, as part of a litany with the rest of the group.

Sharing Words of Praise

After everyone has had time (four to five minutes) to select several verses of praise, invite individuals to read their selected passages. Remember what was suggested earlier—it is better to allow persons to respond and share their passages spontaneously than it is to go around the circle. This is especially true when there is a large group present, and there is not enough time for each one to share the selected verses.

A Litany Response

The passages are read and shared in the spirit of prayer and in the form of a litany. After each passage is read, the whole group responds in unison with a corporate response such as: "O God, hear our prayer of praise, and bless us with your presence." The leader or the group could determine an appropriate response for the group or the setting.

It is the responsibility of the leader to determine when enough persons have shared their Psalm prayers of praise. The appropriate way for the leader to conclude the process is to say, "AMEN!" Let all the people say 'AMEN!' "

Reflecting on the Process

Many persons have difficulty praying extemporaneously in a group setting. For others it is not a threatening experience at all. Those for whom it is an uncomfortable experience often feel guilty that they cannot or prefer not to pray publicly. For these persons and everyone else, it is very nonthreatening to be able to select several verses from a Psalm in order to read them aloud in the group. There is no fear that the words will sound trite or silly because they are words of scripture that are definitely acceptable

to the whole group. It may be that after doing this activity (and others like it), individuals will be able to model their own prayers after the prayers of the Psalmist. I cannot think of any better model. Eventually they may even gain enough courage and confidence to speak their own words in a time of extemporaneous prayer.

A Sample Litany of Praise

I will always thank the Lord;
 I will never stop praising him.
I will praise him for what he has done;
 may all who are oppressed listen and be glad!
Proclaim with me the Lord's greatness;
 let us praise his name together!
Psalm 34:1-3

*Response: O God, hear our prayer of praise
 and bless us with your presence.*

You show your care for the land by sending rain;
 you make it rich and fertile.
You fill the streams with water;
 you provide the earth with crops. . . .
What a rich harvest your goodness provides!
 Wherever you go there is plenty. . . .
Everything shouts and sings for joy.
Psalm 65:9, 11, 13

*Response: O God, hear our prayer of praise
 and bless us with your presence.*

Praise the Lord, my soul!
 All my being, praise his holy name!
Praise the Lord my soul,
 and do not forget how kind he is.
Psalm 103:1-2

*Response: O God, hear our prayer of praise
 and bless us with your presence.*

Praise the Lord, My Soul!
O Lord, my God, how great you are!
You are clothed with majesty and glory;
 you cover yourself with light. . . .
Lord, you have made so many things!
 How wisely you made them all.
 The earth is filled with your creatures. . . .
But when you give them breath, they are created;
 you give new life to the earth.
Psalm 104:1, 2a, 24, 30

*Response: O God, hear our prayer of praise
 and bless us with your presence.*

Prayers of Lament and Supplication

Setting the Stage

We complain about our neighbors, hypocritical church members, the state of the economy, ineffective politicians, and the weather. There are a multitude of persons, systems, organizations, and other subjects that are the focus of our complaints. Seldom in our prayers to God, especially our corporate, public prayers, do we articulate our complaints. This was not true of the Psalmist who often expressed displeasure and despair in the face of evil persons, grief, rejection, and death. These Psalms are classified as Psalms of lament. There are more Psalms of lament than any other single type.

It seems to me that the lamenting Psalms provide a model that may prove valuable as we seek to express our deepest, most honest feelings to God. There are several characteristics of the Psalms of lament that we should keep in mind as we work at expressing our own laments. (Look at chapter 16 in Part Two of this book for a process that guides individuals to identify the characteristics of Psalms of lament. This praying activity may be best used in conjunction with the related teaching activity.) One characteristic is that nothing is withheld from God. The Psalmist addresses God forthrightly and is not bashful about accusing God of being asleep, forgetting his promises, sitting on his hands, or abandoning his people. Such honesty and willingness to tell God how we feel about ourselves, as well as how we feel about God, should be present in our prayers.

A second characteristic is that the laments are accompanied by affirmations of belief in God as the one who creates, judges, loves, forgives, heals, helps, and redeems his people. Believing that God is of this nature enables the Psalmist to address God in confidence and hope, believing that God will respond to the present distress of the individual or the community. We also can approach God with the same belief. Because we believe God to be one who will love and redeem, we can pray with confidence that our prayers will be heard and responded to.

Another characteristic of the Psalms of lament is that for almost every lament there is a corresponding supplication—a petition or request for God to do something particular. In some Psalms there are more verses of lament than supplication, while in other Psalms the opposite is true.

What we will attempt to do in this activity is enable individuals to express their laments—to address God with their deepest hurts, despairs, and troubles. We are accustomed to praying prayers of supplication, but we do not often preface our supplications with our laments as the Psalmist did.

The Leader May Give the Following Guidance to the Experience

The theme verse for this time of praying can best be expressed by Psalm 4:1.

> Answer me when I pray,
>   O God, my defender!
> When I was in trouble, you helped me.
>   Be kind to me now and hear my prayer.

In many Psalms the Psalmist identifies his troubles and brings them to God in prayer. These prayers are known as laments. The Psalmist not only expresses laments but also asks God to respond to the laments. These requests are in the form of prayers of supplication.

To write our own prayers of lament and supplication we need to do two things:
1. Become familiar with some of the Psalmist's laments and supplications.
2. Focus some of our own anger or despair by being specific about what troubles us.

Review Psalms of Lament and Supplication

Let us first look at some representative Psalms to focus on words of lament and supplication. In the next five to eight minutes, read as many of the following passages as you have time. While you read, look specifically for two elements.

1. Look for words of lament, words that express what troubles the Psalmist.
2. Look for words of supplication, words that ask God to do something.

In many instances the lament will be accompanied in the same verse, or later verses, with a corresponding supplication. Notice that some of the laments are of a corporate nature, and others are of the individual.

Read as many of the following Psalms as possible:

1. Psalm 6:1-10
2. Psalm 38:1-22
3. Psalm 41:1-13
4. Psalm 55:1-19
5. Psalm 64:1-10
6. Psalm 69:1-21 and 29-33
7. Psalm 71:1-18
8. Psalm 74:1-23
9. Psalm 88:1-18
10. Psalm 143:1-12

Why have you abandoned us like this, O God?
Will you be angry with your own people forever?
Psalm 74:1

Focus Our Own Laments

You have seen the diversity of the Psalmist's troubles, and you have noticed how direct and honest the Psalmist is in expressing troubles to God as well as requests for God's actions.

Let us spend a few minutes focusing on some causes of the troubles we experience. Think about relationships with persons, situations in the church or community, and affairs of the state, nation, or world. Think also about personal fears, angers, worries, and despairs. Write a list of as many troubles as you can identify in a few minutes. After you have a list, review the list and select the one or two items that trouble you the most—the one or two concerns that you would very much like to express to God. When you have something to focus on, you are prepared to write your own prayer of lament and supplication.

Write Prayers of Lament and Supplication

Using the Psalmist's prayers as a model and focusing on the troubles or concerns that you have identified, write your laments as directly, honestly, and briefly as possible. Address yourself to God, believing that God will not be offended by anything you write. After you have written three or four verses of lament, write three or four corresponding verses of supplication, which ask God to respond to the needs you have expressed. Take about five minutes to write.

Pray the Prayers

Because of the very personal nature of many of the prayers, it may be best to not expect individuals to share their prayers by reading them aloud. It will be sufficient to direct everyone to read their prayers silently. Suggest that the prayers be read slowly and with feeling, believing that God hears the spoken as well as the unspoken prayers.

Closure

As a means of closure, invite all the participants to read or recite in unison the Twenty-third Psalm.

5

The Mighty Acts of God

Setting the Stage

There are four Psalms that can be clearly identified as salvation history Psalms (Psalms 78, 105, 106, 136). These Psalms, for the most part, are written in the form of a narrative presenting events, the mighty acts of God, in a chronological order. The four Psalms each include a different combination of God's acts—the earliest being the act of creation (Psalm 136) and the latest being the anointing of David as king (Psalm 78). For a teaching activity that explores this psalm type in some depth, see chapter 14 on "Psalms of the Mighty Acts." It may be profitable to experience the teaching activity before engaging in the praying activity. If this is not possible, it would be helpful for the leader to provide some introduction to the characteristics of the salvation history Psalms.

It is quite possible that the salvation history Psalms were used for didactic as well as liturgical purposes. Psalm 78 has a prologue that clearly states the didactic purpose of the Psalm.

> Listen, my people, to my teaching,
>   and pay attention to what I say.
> I am going to use wise sayings
>   and explain mysteries from the past,
>   things we have heard and known,
>   things that our [parents] told us.
> We will not keep them from our children;
>   we will tell the next generation
>   about the Lord's power and his great deeds
>   and the wonderful things he has done. . . .
> He gave laws to the people of Israel
>   and commandments to the descendants
>   of Jacob.
> He instructed our ancestors to teach his laws
>   to their children,
> so that the next generation might learn them
>   and in turn should tell their children.
>
> Psalm 78:1-6

What follows in the remaining sixty-six verses is a remembering of God's great deeds, his mighty acts, from the Exodus out of Egypt to the choosing of David as king. No doubt this Psalm was remembered and recited often in the informal and formal settings of instruction and worship.

Psalm 136, on the other hand, is composed in the form of a litany. There are twenty-six verses, each one in two parts with an affirmation of an act of God followed by the response, "For his steadfast love endures for ever" (RSV). This Psalm begins with God's act of creation and concludes with the Israelites settling in the land of Canaan following the desert pilgrimage from Egypt. Written in the form of a litany, the Psalm probably was used in the context of worship with a choir or the congregation singing the refrain in response to the priestly choir or a single priest.

With Psalm 136 in the form of a litany, we will use that Psalm as the basis and the form for the sequence of litanies that will be written and shared in this praying activity.

Leading the Activity

Introduce the activity by describing the nature of salvation history Psalms and reviewing briefly the steps of the activity.

Pray Psalm 136 as a Litany

The leader could read the first line of each verse with the group reading the response. Or other variations could be utilized:

1. men reading the first line with women responding,
2. women reading the first line with men responding,
3. one-half of the group reading the first line and the other half responding to it,
4. someone singing the first line and the group responding,
5. or use a combination of the above with the leader giving cues to the group.

27

Regarding the response: the response in the TEV is, "his love is eternal"; in the Jewish translation *(The Book of Psalms)*, the response is, "his steadfast love is eternal"; and in the RSV the response is "his steadfast love endures for ever." Any one of the responses would be appropriate. However, I have found that the RSV response works better; it is the most familiar and is not as flat or abbreviated as the other two.

Writing Statements

Using the form of Psalm 136, with its very brief, affirmative statements describing the mighty acts of God, invite the participants to write similar statements focused on God's mighty acts through Jesus the Christ and his faithful followers in the early church.

After giving participants three to four minutes to write one or two lines, invite them to share what they have written. When a line is read, the group responds with the refrain used previously with Psalm 136.

In a sense this step is a chance to practice the form. The leader is able to determine whether or not the participants understood the directions. The participants are able to practice the process of writing, sharing their statements, and responding with the refrain. If there are any difficulties, the leader can make suggestions to the group before going any further.

Writing Additional Statements

In this step the participants will write brief statements on three additional topics or aspects of the mighty acts of God in relation to:

1. the history of the church,
2. the life of the church in the world today,
3. or one's own life experiences.

It would be most helpful if each participant received a worksheet (see page 29).

Sharing

After writing there needs to be some time provided for sharing the statements in the form of a litany. All the statements for each item should be shared before going on to the next. The personal expressions will then conclude the litany.

Reflecting on the Process

The whole activity may take as long as thirty minutes. If one or more of the process elements were omitted, the activity could be accomplished in less time. The problem with omitting an element is that something significant will be missing from a whole process, a process which attempts to provide linkage between the mighty acts of God in the midst of the people, Israel, and the mighty acts of God in our lives today.

When all of the statements from Psalm 136 plus the other four elements are seen as part of a whole process, all who have participated will have made a grand affirmation of their faith in God—as one who has acted for the restoration and redemption of the people in every generation of creation. One participant said to me after experiencing this activity, "It had never occurred to me that I could think of what was happening in the world today and in my life as being similar to God's mighty acts that I have read about in the Bible."

This praying activity would be especially appropriate in conjunction with celebrating the anniversary of a church, as part of a church history study, or as part of study and action demonstrating that working for peace and justice today is consistent with God's mighty acts.

The Mighty Acts of God

Read Psalm 136 again. After each of the following statements, write one or two lines (verses) in the same form as Psalm 136, focusing the lines on the subject of each statement.

1. With God's people . . . the first followers and disciples of Jesus.

2. With God's people . . . the church throughout history.

3. With God's people . . . the church today.

4. With God's people . . . we who are gathered today in this place.

6

Praise the Lord, My Soul!

As for us, our life is like grass.
We grow and flourish like a wild flower;
    then the wind blows on it, and it is gone—
    no one sees it again.
But for those who honor the Lord,
    his love lasts forever,
    and his goodness endures for all generations.

Psalm 103:15-17

Setting the Stage

Psalm 103 is one of those priceless treasures that becomes more precious as we spend time with it in reflection and contemplation. The Psalm has four main parts:

1. Personal blessings received from God (1-5).
2. National blessings received from God (6-14).
3. A reminder of our human frailty and utter dependence upon God (15-18).
4. A declaration that all creation praises God (19-22).

The Psalm begins with words of praise for God's blessings—forgiveness of sin, healing from disease, redemption from death, surrounding with love and renewal of life. In response to these blessings from God, how can anyone, Psalmist or ourselves, do anything but offer words of praise and thanksgiving? This response is accented by the repeated phrase, "Bless the Lord, O my soul" and reinforced by "all that is within me" (RSV). All that a person is and has is offered to God in praise and thanksgiving for God's great blessings.

The second part of the Psalm moves from the personal to the corporate or national experience of God's grace. As a representative of the people, the Psalmist reminds all who will listen and believe that God judges in favor of the oppressed, God reveals plans to and through the chosen leaders, God is always merciful, loving, and forgiving, and God remembers who we are and what we are made of. For all of God's graciousness through these mighty acts, the Psalmist again exclaims with words of praise and thanksgiving.

The third part is an extension or illumination of the verse, "He knows what we are made of; he remembers that we are dust" (14). Life is cyclical; it grows like the grass and the flowers in the spring and summer, and with the winds of the winter it is gone. Persons and nations are born; they flourish and they die. Although this is the nature of persons and nations, it is not the nature of God's love. God's love lasts forever—God's goodness endures through all the generations of those who are faithful to God's covenant.

Praise God for blessings to the person. Praise God for blessings to the nation. Praise God for

continued faithfulness to those who keep the covenant. And, as in the last section, praise God all the creation, the angels, the heavenly powers, all his creatures—Praise the Lord!

Psalm 103, as a beautiful hymn of praise, is worth spending some time with to let it speak to us today. In this activity we are going to experience the words, images, and meanings of the Psalm in a variety of ways. What at first may appear to be dull repetition can become a moving experience of relating to the Psalm in more and more depth.

The activity as outlined includes seven different forms, or "translations," of the Psalm. The total activity will require twenty or more minutes. It is possible to shorten the activity by omitting one or more of the translations. It is also possible to lengthen the activity by providing time for silence, reading an additional translation, or singing another hymn.

Guiding the Participants in the Experience

Before presenting Psalm 103 in its several forms, it is helpful to review the Psalm briefly with participants looking at the Psalm in their Bibles while the leader points out the four distinct parts of the Psalm as presented in the above section.

Read and Listen to Three Translations

After the leader briefly reviews the parts of the Psalm and calls attention to the blessings of God worthy of our praise, the participants are ready to hear the Psalm read in three different translations. The three translations are (see bibliography):

1. *THE BOOK OF PSALMS* (Jewish translation)
2. *THE JERUSALEM BIBLE* (Roman Catholic translation)
3. *GOOD NEWS BIBLE* (Protestant translation)

Other translations could be substituted for or added to those recommended.

It is important to select three good readers with a mix of voices—male, female, younger, older, etc.

The readings will be done of the Psalm in the sequence listed below. Readers will read one portion at a time for all translations and then repeat the process for the next portion.

The portions are:

1. Verses 1-5   4. Verses 15-18
2. Verses 6-10   5. Verses 19-22
3. Verses 11-14

Encourage members of the group, as they listen to the several translations, to listen carefully for significant as well as subtle differences in the translations.

View a Filmstrip

A fifth way to present Psalm 103 is by the use of a filmstrip (see chapter 7 and the bibliography for additional information regarding the filmstrip). In a series of five filmstrips called *Psalm Prayers,* Psalm 103 is included. Even though the series is intended for children, the filmstrip is appropriate for youth and adults. In fact, youth and adults may appreciate the filmstrip more than the children.

The filmstrip should be set up ahead of time—focused, ready with the first frame, and tape set at the right spot with the volume already adjusted. This preparation is important so that immediately after hearing the three translations read, the leader can introduce the filmstrip, turn off the lights, and turn on the projector and recorder.

Sing a Hymn

After viewing the filmstrip, the group can be led in singing a hymn based upon Psalm 103. There are several hymns that find their origin in Psalm 103. Refer to the scripture index found in the back of most hymnbooks, and you will find some appropriate hymns. Some possible hymns include:

1. "Bless, O My Soul! The Living God"
2. "Joyful, Joyful, We Adore Thee"
3. "Praise to the Lord, the Almighty"
4. "There's a Wideness in God's Mercy"

Read from *Psalms/Now*

A way to close the activity is to read Leslie Brandt's meditation on Psalm 103 from his book *Psalms-Now* (see bibliography). His meditation captures much of the meaning of the Psalm with quite contemporary words and images. Individuals may identify with these images out of their own personal experiences.

7

Five Psalm Prayers—A Filmstrip Series

Setting the Stage

In presenting this activity, I realize I am recommending a resource that may not be immediately available to many church groups. However, the resource, a set of five filmstrips entitled *Psalm Prayers* (see bibliography for details) is so outstanding that I would like to encourage churches to borrow, rent, or purchase it where possible. Many media resource centers, especially Catholic diocesan resource centers often have the set of filmstrips available for loan or rental. It is also possible for a cluster of churches to cooperatively purchase a variety of resources, thus not duplicating titles and sharing what they have with each other.

Each filmstrip focuses on a different Psalm. The filmstrip titles and the five Psalms are:

1. *Loneliness*—Psalm 31
2. *Peace*—Psalm 32
3. *Joy*—Psalm 103
4. *Security*—Psalm 121
5. *Gratitude*—Psalm 138

The filmstrips are designed to be used primarily with children. For that reason the subjects of each frame are children, and the experiences that are used as illustrations are experiences of children. This is one of the few audio-visual resources on Psalms I know of that is appropriate for children. The emotions, concepts, images, and expressions, although intended for children, are quite appropriate for youth and adults. The presentations are very much focused on common life experiences that we all remember from our own childhoods—experiences that we can apply to the more mature experiences of our present lives and that as teachers, parents, friends, or relatives of children, we can identify with personally.

Each filmstrip follows a similar format. The first twenty frames present some common life experiences that set the stage for understanding the intention of the writer of the Psalm. There is a transitional frame or two that says, "That is why I pray to you, Lord; hear me, Lord, as I pray this psalm. . . ." Then follows another twenty frames, the text of which is an appropriate paraphrase of the Psalm with a vocabulary that can be understood by everyone.

Instead of outlining one activity, I will suggest several ways the filmstrips can be used in the context of congregational worship or group devotions.

Congregational Worship

When the lectionary calls for one of the five Psalms or when the leader of worship selects one of the five Psalms (31, 32, 103, 121, and 138), the filmstrip could be projected and viewed instead of reading the Psalm from the Bible. In order to do this, it would be necessary to darken the room where the service of worship is conducted, or arrangements could be made for a rear projection screen that allows for satisfactory viewing in a space that cannot be darkened adequately. It will also be necessary to have an adequate sound system or large enough speaker attachment to the cassette tape recorder in order to amplify the sound so that everyone could hear the narration without difficulty.

If a congregation is not accustomed to experiencing audio-visuals in the context of a service of worship, then you will want to introduce the filmstrip and the process carefully. Many churches include a children's sermon or some such time for children in the early part of the service. Often it is possible to introduce new resources or elements of worship for the children, with adults observing eagerly. Eventually it is possible to use the same resources or elements with the adults without too many negative reactions.

Youth or Adult Bible Study

For youth or adult Bible study, focus on any one of the five Psalms. After studying the Psalm, the group can view the whole filmstrip. Group members can then spend some time paraphrasing selected verses (each member with a different verse or two so that all the verses of the Psalm are included). When the paraphrases are completed, the second half of the filmstrip can be shown with individuals reading their own paraphrases for the appropriate filmstrip frames. This activity can be in the form of a closing prayer, illustrated with projected photographs.

Activities with Children

As part of a church school or catechism class, there can be a time of prayer during which a filmstrip from the *Psalm Prayers* series will be used. There can be a brief call to worship with a verse or two from a Psalm, followed by a reading (perhaps in unison) of the Psalm that the filmstrip is based on. After reading the Psalm the leader can introduce the filmstrip, followed by the group viewing the filmstrip in an attitude of prayer.

Meetings or Other Gatherings

Many committees and boards of churches begin their meetings with brief devotions. Also, may other groups in the church such as couples, singles, men, or women have monthly meetings where a brief experience of worship is part of the agenda. Any one of the *Psalm Prayers* filmstrips or all of them in a series are appropriate as a theme for worship. It is quite easy to build a brief service around the filmstrips, which would include a call to worship, a reading of the Psalm (in unison or responsively), viewing the filmstrip, singing a hymn based upon the Psalm, or related to the theme of the Psalm, and closing with a spontaneous litany where participants offer their own phrases or sentences of prayer.

8

Forms of Reading/Praying the Psalms

Setting the Stage

Written in a poetic form the Psalms are composed of brief phrases and lines where one line reinforces another, responds to another, or is in contrast to another. In this form, plus the experiential content and the address to God, the Psalms are a natural resource for inclusion in corporate worship. One who is familiar with the Psalms will notice that most services of congregational worship include Psalm references in one or more parts of the service: calls to worship, invocations, hymns, prayers, scripture readings, responsive readings, sermon references, or benedictions.

The tradition of including portions of Psalms in congregational worship is an ancient tradition beginning with the temple worship of the people of Israel, and throughout the history of the Christian church. Psalms were an important part of the spiritual disciplines of the monastic communities and continue to be so today for all who maintain the disciplined practice of prayer and scripture reading.

In this activity I will suggest seven different forms that can be considered and utilized when planning for corporate worship. One form can be used by itself as a brief opening prayer for a meeting, or several forms can be interspersed in a more formal service of worship. All of the

Happy are those whose sins are forgiven,
  whose wrongs are pardoned. . . .
I confessed my sins to you;
  I did not conceal my wrongdoings.
I decided to confess them to you,
  and you forgave all my sins.

Psalm 32:1, 5

forms are designed to involve the participants with the Psalms.

Unison Reading

In some hymnbooks there are Psalms selected and recommended for unison reading. Any church that has Bibles, along with hymnbooks and/or prayerbooks in the pews, can involve the worshipers in unison reading of a Psalm or other passage of scripture. It is also possible to print Psalm texts in the bulletin that contains the order of worship. In groups that meet regularly for study, business or fellowship, Bibles can be provided so that everyone is able to participate in a unison reading.

Some suggested Psalm passages that are appropriate for reading in unison include:

1. For a prayer of invocation:
   Psalm 40:1-8, Psalm 63:1-5, and Psalm 92:1-4
2. For a prayer of confession:
   Psalm 25:1-2, Psalm 40:12-17, and Psalm 51:1-17
3. For a prayer of trust:
   Psalm 16:1-11, Psalm 23:1-6, and Psalm 131:1-3
4. For a prayer of praise and thanksgiving:
   Psalm 65:1-7, Psalm 113:1-9, and Psalm 138:1-8
5. For an affirmation of faith in God:
   Psalm 46:1-11, Psalm 62:1-7, and Psalm 111:1-10

Responsive Reading

Many of the Psalms lend themselves to being read responsively. Reading responsively occurs when a leader reads one line, and the worshipers respond by reading the second line. As with unison readings there are many hymnbooks that include responsive readings of the Psalms and other portions of scripture. Also, if Bibles are in the pews, it is possible to select Psalms to read responsively other than the ones in the hymnbook.

Antiphonal Reading

Passages selected for responsive readings are also appropriate for antiphonal readings. An-tiphonal means "answering responsively." An antiphonal reading is different from a responsive reading in that one *group* reads and another *group* responds antiphonally, rather than one person reading with a group responding. In antiphonal readings it is possible for the choir to read one line, with the congregation reading the next line. Or, one side of the gathered congregation reads one line to which the other side responds with the second line.

Some suggested Psalms that are appropriate for both responsive and antiphonal readings:

1. For a call to worship:
   Psalm 15:1-5, Psalm 24:3-10, Psalm 50:1-6, and Psalm 134:1-3.
2. For a call to prayer:
   Psalm 32:1-5, Psalm 61:1-5, and Psalm 103:1-5.
3. For a prayer of praise:
   Psalm 95:1-7, Psalm 98:1-9, Psalm 100:1-5, and Psalm 148:1-14
4. For affirming belief in God:
   Psalm 111:1-10, Psalm 113:1-9, and Psalm 121:1-8
5. For introducing the reading of scripture:
   Psalm 19:7-11, Psalm 78:1-7, Psalm 119:33-40, and Psalm 119:105-112

Litany

A litany is a series of statements read by a leader to which the worshipers answer with a brief response. Ordinarily the same response is repeated throughout the entire litany or at least for several statements. Another brief response may be used after several more statements. Psalm 136 is a good example of a litany that is present among the Psalms. It is possible to add a litany response after each line of some of the Psalms of praise such as Psalms 146, 148, or 150. A response such as, "Thanks be to God" or "O God, be present with us" is appropriate.

Lining the Psalms

When additional Bibles or the printed text of a Psalm are not available for the prticipants to read along with the leader, there is another way to involve the participants in speaking the words of the Psalm. This process can be described as lining out the Psalms. The leader reads or chants a line, and the worshipers repeat the line. The leader is able to cue the response of the people by use of the voice, with pace, volume, and tone. The lining process should be used with a limited number of verses of a Psalm, so that the interest and involvement of the people are not overextended.

Choral Reading

Choral reading is another way to involve persons in reading/praying the Psalms. It is important for the leader to plan carefully in advance and to duplicate the text with clearly marked lines giving the necessary cues for the readers. Choral reading can be a dramatic, moving way to involve all or some of the participants. Two examples of choral readings are presented as illustrations. A similar treatment of other selected Psalms could be planned by pastors or educators. Taking the time to group people according to the pitches of their speaking voices can add to the power of the Psalm reading, but this grouping is not absolutely necessary for the activity to be meaningful.

Psalm 66

All: Praise God with shouts of joy, all people!

Group 1: Sing to the glory of his name; offer him glorious praise!

Group 2: Say to God, "How wonderful are the things you do!
Your power is so great that your enemies bow down in fear before you.

Group 3: Everyone on earth worships you; they sing praises to you, they sing praises to your name."

Group 1: Come and see what God has done, his wonderful acts among [humankind].

Group 2: He changed the sea into dry land; our ancestors crossed the river on foot.
There we rejoiced because of what he did.

Group 3: He rules forever by his might and keeps his eyes on the nations.

Let no rebels rise against him.

All: Praise our God, all nations; let your praise be heard.
He has kept us alive and has not allowed us to fall.

Group 1: You have put us to the test, God; as silver is purified by fire, so you have tested us.

Group 2: You let us fall into a trap and placed heavy burdens on our backs.

Group 3: You let our enemies trample us; we went through fire and flood,

All: but now you have brought us to a place of safety.

Reader 1: I will bring burnt offerings to your house;

Reader 2: I will offer you what I promised.

Reader 3: I will give you what I said I would when I was in trouble. . . .

Readers 1, 2, and 3: Come and listen, all who honor God,
and I will tell you what he has done for me.

Reader 1: I cried to him for help; I praised him with songs.

Reader 2: If I had ignored my sins, the Lord would not have listened to me.

Reader 3: But God has indeed heard me; he has listened to my prayer.

Readers 1, 2, and 3: I praise God,
because he did not reject my prayer
or keep back his constant love for me.

Psalm 103

Group 1: Praise the Lord, my soul!
All my being, praise his holy name!

Group 2: Praise the Lord, my soul, and do not forget how kind he is.

Reader 1: He forgives all my sins

Reader 2: and heals all my diseases.

Reader 3: He keeps me from the grave

Reader 4: and blesses me with love and
mercy.

Reader 5: He fills my life with good things,
so that I stay young and strong
like an eagle.

Group 1: The Lord judges in favor of the
oppressed
and gives them their rights.

Group 2: [The Lord] revealed his plans to
Moses
and let the people of Israel see his
mighty deeds.

Group 1: The Lord is merciful and loving,
slow to become angry and full of
constant love.

He does not keep on rebuking;
he is not angry forever.

Group 2: He does not punish us as we
deserve
or repay us according to our sins
and wrongs.

Group 1: As high as the sky is above the
earth,

Group 2: so great is his love for those who
honor him.

Group 1: As far as the east is from the west,

Group 2: so far does he remove our sins
from us.

Group 1: As a father is kind to his children,

Group 2: so the Lord is kind to those who
honor him.

All: He knows what we are made of;
he remembers that we are dust.
As for us, our life is like grass.

Group 1: We grow and flourish like a wild
flower;
then the wind blows on it,
and it is gone—
no one sees it again.

Group 2: But for those who honor the Lord,
his love lasts forever,
and his goodness endures
for all generations
of those who are true to his
covenant
and who faithfully obey his
commands.

All: The Lord placed his throne in
heaven;
he is king over all.

Group 1: Praise the Lord, you strong and
mighty angels,
who obey his commands,
who listen to what he says.

Group 2: Praise the Lord, all you heavenly
powers,
you servants of his, who do his
will!

All: Praise the Lord, all his creatures
in all the places he rules.
Praise the Lord, my soul!

Silent Reading

If there are selected Psalm texts available for
each participant to read, it is appropriate to
provide a time for individuals to read recommended Psalms silently. Let the participants
choose which one(s) they will read. Or, a specific
Psalm can be printed in the order of service with
a time of silence provided for everyone to read,
reflect, and respond personally to that Psalm.
Very few minutes of a sixty-minute worship
service are devoted to silence. Some persons are
threatened by silence, but with encouragement
and practice, the moments of silence can become
a very meaningful aspect of the worship
experience.

9

A Liturgy of Psalms

Setting the Stage

We have already considered the fact that in their original use, the Psalms were included as part of the worship of God's people—Israel as well as the Christian church. The variety of types of Psalms provides for some to be especially appropriate as calls to worship, prayers of confession, prayers of thanksgiving, hymns of praise, and other elements of worship. In chapter 8, we identified particular Psalms as appropriate for unison, responsive, and antiphonal readings for the various parts of worship. As I have lived with the Psalms these past several years, I have come to realize that it is possible to plan a complete liturgy, featuring the Psalms and including all the traditional elements of worship. However, there is something essential missing from Christian worship that focuses exclusively on the Psalms—a witness to the life, death, and resurrection of Jesus, God's messiah for all people. It is important not to omit this Gospel witness, yet is it possible to use the Psalms as a basis for a liturgy that also includes proclamation of the Good News of God's mighty acts in and through Jesus Christ and his body, the church.

The liturgy presented in this activity could be used in almost any setting of corporate worship. If it is used as a regular Sunday morning service, worshipers should be prepared by articles in the church newsletter, announcements in the weekly bulletin, and/or an introduction at the beginning of the service. The service would be especially meaningful if it were the occasion for recognition of the choirs in late spring. A variety of hymns and anthems based upon the Psalms could be incorporated in the service, thus providing ample opportunity for participation by all the choirs. I had the pleasure of attending such a service, a Psalm festival, at the Ginter Park Presbyterian Church in Richmond, Virginia.

In the liturgy that follows I have included the words of most of the Psalms in order to provide the reader with a sense of the flow of the liturgy. If Bibles are available to all worshipers, the words of the Psalms need not be reprinted in the order of service.

A Liturgy of Psalms

Choral Introit   "O Come and Sing Unto the Lord"
           (A hymn based upon Psalm 95)

O come and sing unto the Lord,
To him our voices raise;
Let us in our most joyful songs
The Lord, our Savior, praise.

Call to Worship   (Responsively)
      Psalm 113 (selected verses)

All: Praise the Lord!
  L: You servants of the Lord, praise his name!
  P: May his name be praised, now and forever.
  L: From the east to the west
  P: praise the name of the Lord! . . .
  L: There is no one like the Lord our God.
  P: He lives in the heights above . . .
  L: He raises the poor from the dust;
  P: he lifts the needy from their misery . . .
All: Praise the Lord!

Prayer of Invocation   (Unison)
      Psalm 63:1-15

O God, you are my God, and I long for you.
My whole being desires you;
    like a dry, worn-out, and waterless land,
    my soul is thirsty for you.
Let me see you in the sanctuary;
    let me see how mighty and glorious you are.
Your constant love is better than life itself,
    and so I will praise you.

I will give you thanks as long as I live;
I will raise my hands to you in prayer.
My soul will feast and be satisfied,
  and I will sing glad songs of praise to you.

Hymn of Praise
  "All People That on Earth Do Dwell"
  (A hymn based upon Psalm 100)

All people that on earth do dwell,
Sing to the Lord with cheerful voice.
Him serve with mirth, his praise forth tell;
Come ye before him and rejoice.

Know that the Lord is God indeed;
Without our aid he did us make;
We are his folk, he doth us feed,
And for his sheep he doth us take.

Prayer of Confession   (Unison)
  Psalm 51:1-5, 10-12, 16-17

Be merciful to me, O God, because of your
  constant love.
Because of your great mercy wipe away my
  sins!
Wash away all my evil and make me clean
  from my sin!
I recognize my faults; I am always conscious of
  my sins.
I have sinned against you—only against
  you—and done what you consider evil.
So you are right in judging me; you are
  justified in condemning me.
I have been evil from the time I was born;
from the time I was conceived, I have been
  sinful.
reate a pure heart in me, O God,
  and put a new and loyal spirit in me.
Do not banish me from your presence.
  do not take your Holy Spirit away from me.
Give me again the joy that comes from your
  salvation,
and make me willing to obey you.

You do not want sacrifices, or I would offer
  them;
you are not pleased with burnt offerings.
My sacrifice is a humble spirit, O God;
you will not reject a humble and repentant
  heart.
                                        Amen

Assurance of Pardon   (Responsively)
  Psalm 32

(From Psalm 32 as paraphrased in the second
stanza of the hymn "How Blest Is He Whose
Trespass")

L: When I kept guilty silence,
      my strength was spent with grief;
P: Thy hand was heavy on me,
      my soul found no relief;
L: But when I owned my trespass,
      my sin hid not from thee;
P: When I confessed transgression,
      then thou forgavest me.
L: Friends, let us live as those
      who believe the Good News;
P: In Jesus Christ, we are forgiven.

Introduction to Reading Scripture Psalm 78:1-7

(Read by the leader)

Listen, my people, to my teaching,
  and pay attention to what I say.
I am going to use wise sayings
  and explain mysteries from the past,
  things we have heard and known,
  things that our [parents] told us.
We will not keep them from our children;
  we will tell the next generation
  about the Lord's power and his great deeds
  and the wonderful things he has done.
He gave laws to the people of Israel
  and commandments to the descendents of
    Jacob.
He instructed our ancestors
  to teach his laws to their children,
so that the next generation might learn them
  and in turn should tell their children.
In this way they also will put their trust in God
  and not forget what he has done,
  but always obey his commandments.

Old Testament Lesson   (Unison)

  Deuteronomy 26:5-9

In the Lord's presence you will recite these
words; "My ancestor was a wandering Aramean, who took his family to Egypt to live.
They were few in number when they went

there, but they became a large and powerful nation. The Egyptians treated us harshly and forced us to work as slaves. Then we cried out for help to the Lord, the God of our ancestors. He heard us and saw our suffering, hardship, and misery. By his great power and strength he rescued us from Egypt. He worked miracles and wonders, and caused terrifying things to happen. He brought us here and gave us this rich and fertile land."

Psalm Response   (Lined out by the leader)

Psalm 34 (selected verses)

Proclaim with me the Lord's greatness;
    let us praise his name together! . . .
The Lord watches over the righteous
    and listens to their cries . . .
The righteous call to the Lord,
    and he listens;
he rescues them from all their troubles.
The Lord is near to those who are
    discouraged;
he saves those who have lost all hope. . . .
The Lord will save his people.

New Testament Lesson   (Read by the leader)

Ephesians 2:4-10

But God's mercy is so abundant, and his love for us is so great, that while we were spiritually dead in our disobedience he brought us to life with Christ. It is by God's grace that you have been saved. In our union with Christ Jesus he raised us up with him to rule with him in the heavenly world. He did this to demonstrate for all time to come the extraordinary greatness of his grace in the love he showed us in Christ Jesus. For it is by God's grace that you have been saved through faith. It is not the result of your own efforts, but God's gift, so that no one can boast about it. God has made us what we are, and in our union with Christ Jesus he has created us for a life of good deeds, which he has already prepared for us to do.

Psalm Response   (Lined out by the leader)

Psalm 62:1, 5-8

I wait patiently for God to save me . . .
I depend on God alone,
I put my hope in him.
He alone protects and saves me;
    he is my defender . . .
My salvation and honor depend on God . . .
Trust in God at all times, my people.

Interpreting the Scriptures

The leader of worship will present a brief homily, which speaks about the nature of Psalms and emphasizes the message of hope and salvation proclaimed by the Psalmist and fulfilled by the life, death, and resurrection of Jesus the Christ.

Affirmation of Faith   (Unison)

Psalm 111:1-4, 7-10

Praise the Lord!
With all my heart I will thank the Lord
    in the assembly of his people.
How wonderful are the things the Lord does!
All who are delighted with them
    want to understand them.
All he does is full of honor and majesty;
    his righteousness is eternal.
The Lord does not let us forget his wonderful
    actions;
    he is kind and merciful. . . .
In all he does [the Lord] is faithful and just;
    all his commands are dependable.
They last for all time;
    they were given in truth and righteousness.
He set his people free
    and made an eternal covenant with them.
Holy and mighty is [the Lord]!
The way to become wise is to honor the
    Lord . . .
He is to be praised forever.
[Praise the Lord!]

Prayers of the People

The worship leader may offer prayers in the style of the Psalms or advance preparations may involve some of the worshipers in composing brief prayers in the style of the Psalms. Members may offer their prayers from where they are sitting in the congregation.

42

Offertory Anthem

The organist and/or choir director may select an anthem for choirs. An anthem based upon Psalm 150 would be an excellent choice. It might be possible to have the instruments mentioned in the Psalm accompany the singing, and one or more dancers could interpret the Psalm through dance and movement.

Hymn of Commitment

"A Mighty Fortress Is Our God"

(Hymn based upon Psalm 46)

Charge to the Congregation   Psalm 31:23, 24

Love the Lord, all his faithful people.
The Lord protects the faithful . . .

Be strong, be courageous,
    all you who hope in the Lord.

Benediction   Colossians 3:15-17

The peace that Christ gives is to guide you in the decisions you make; for it is to this peace that God has called you together in the one body. And be thankful. Christ's message in all its richness must live in your hearts. Teach and instruct one another with all wisdom. Sing psalms, hymns, and sacred songs; sing to God with thanksgiving in your hearts. Everything you do or say, then, should be done in the name of the Lord Jesus, as you give thanks through him to God the Father.   Amen!

10

An Informal Liturgy of Psalms

Setting the Stage

The previous praying activity was planned for a more formal one-hour service of worship. The elements of this liturgy are quite flexible and can be reduced or expanded depending upon the setting, the amount of time, and the number of persons participating. The example that follows is a product of a class I taught recently. These folks spent about twenty hours together in a conference setting, where in one week we were able to explore and experience a wide variety of praying and teaching activities with the Psalms. As part of a teaching activity we identified twelve parts of a liturgy. The parts were divided among the participants so that each participant, some in pairs or small groups, was responsible for selecting a Psalm, portion of a Psalm, or portions of two or more Psalms that would be both appropriate to the part of worship and appropriate to the theme of the service, "God is

Creator, Lord and Redeemer." As they worked on the assignment, in addition to selecting appropriate Psalms, they were to determine in which form the Psalm(s) could be presented.

The twelve elements of the liturgy that the class members worked with were:
1. Preparing for worship (a Psalm for personal meditation)
2. Call to worship
3. Prayer of invocation (or praise)
4. Hymns (two or three hymns for praise, thanksgiving, and trust)
5. Prayers of confession (individual) and assurance of pardon
6. Prayer of lament of the community
7. Remembering God's great deeds
8. Prayers of petition
9. Words of promise and hope
10. Psalms and the Gospel message
11. Prayers of thanksgiving
12. Benediction

The order of the liturgy was as listed above except for the hymns. The three hymns were interspersed throughout the liturgy.

What follows are the words of the Psalms that were selected and shared together in an informal liturgy. Approximately twenty persons were present, and the complete liturgy required about thirty minutes. This liturgy can be shared with a group just as it is, or the group can go through the same process we did in order to prepare its own liturgy.

An Informal Liturgy of Psalms:

Celebrating God as Creator, Lord, and Redeemer

Preparing for Worship   Psalm 139:1-6
    (A Psalm for personal meditation)

Lord, you have examined me and you know me.
You know everything I do;
    from far away you understand all my thoughts.
You see me, whether I am working or resting;
    you know all my actions.
Even before I speak,
    you already know what I will say.
You are all around me on every side;
    you protect me with your power.
Your knowledge of me is too deep;
    it is beyond my understanding.

(Suggest that Psalm 139:1-6 be read silently by the participants and meditated upon for about five minutes to prepare for worship.)

Call to Worship   (Responsively)
        Psalm 95:1-2, 6-7

L: Come, let us praise the Lord!
P: Let us sing for joy to God, who protects us!
L: Let us come before him with thanksgiving
P: and sing joyful songs of praise.
L: Come, let us bow down and worship him;
P: let us kneel before the Lord, our Maker!
L: He is our God;
P: we are the people he cares for.

Prayer of Invocation   (Unison)
        Psalm 8 (paraphrased)

O Lord, our Lord,
    your greatness is seen in all the world! . . .
When I look at the sky, which you have made,

at the moon and the stars, which you set in
    their places,—
Who am I, that you think of me;
    mere human, that you care for me?
Yet you have made me inferior only to yourself,
    you have crowned me with glory and honor.
O Lord, our Lord,
    your greatness is seen in all the world!

Hymns   (These three hymns are to be sung at
        appropriate times in the liturgy)

A Hymn of Praise   Psalms 103 and 150
    "Praise to the Lord, the Almighty"

A Hymn of Thanksgiving   Psalm 30
    "O Lord, by Thee Delivered"

A Hymn of Trust   Psalm 90
    "O God, Our Help in Ages Past"

Prayer of Confession   (Unison)
        Psalm 25 (selected verses)

To you, O Lord, I offer my prayer;
    in you, my God, I trust. . . .
Keep your promise, Lord, and forgive my sins,
    for they are many. . . .
Turn to me, Lord, and be merciful to me,
    because I am lonely and weak. . . .
Consider my distress and suffering
    and forgive all my sins. . . .
Teach me your ways, O Lord;
    make them known to me.
Teach me to live according to your truth,
    for you are my God, who saves me.
I always trust in you.

Assurance of Pardon   (Read by leader)
        Psalm 32:1-2, 11

Happy are those whose sins are forgiven,
    whose wrongs are pardoned. . . .
Happy is the [one] whom the Lord does not
    accuse of doing wrong and who is free from
    all deceit. . . .
You that are righteous, be glad and rejoice
    because of what the Lord has done. Amen!

Community Prayers of Lament (Antiphonally)
        Psalm 90

A. O Lord, you have always been our home.

B. Before you created the hills
or brought the world into being,
you were eternally God,
and will be God forever. . . .

A. A thousand years to you are like one day;
they are like yesterday, already gone,
like a short hour in the night. . . .

B. We are like weeds that sprout in the morning,
that grow and burst into bloom,
then dry up and die in the evening.

A. We are destroyed by your anger.
we are terrified by your fury.

B. You place our sins before you,
our secret sins where you can see
them. . . .

A. How much longer will your anger last?
Have pity, O Lord, on your servants!

B. Fill us each morning with your constant love,
so that we may sing and be glad all our life.

A. Give us now as much happiness as the sadness
you gave us during all our years of misery.

B. Let us, your servants, see your mighty deeds;
let our descendants see your glorious [strength].

ALL: Lord, our God, may your blessings be with us.

Remembering God's Great Deeds
(As a litany)   Psalm 146

ALL: Praise the Lord!
Praise the Lord, my soul!
L: I will praise [the Lord] as long as I live;
I will sing to my God all my life.
P: Praise the Lord!
L: Don't put your trust in human leaders;
no human being can save you.
P: Praise the Lord!
L: When they die, they return to the dust;
on that day all their plans come to an end.

P: Praise the Lord!
L: Happy is the [one] who has the God of Jacob to help him
and who depends on the Lord his God,
the Creator of heaven, earth, and sea,
and all that is in them.
P: Praise the Lord!
L: He always keeps his promises;
he judges in favor of the oppressed
and gives food to the hungry.
P: Praise the Lord!
L: The Lord sets prisoners free
and gives sight to the blind.
P: Praise the Lord!
L: The Lord lifts those who have fallen;
he loves his righteous people.
P: Praise the Lord!
L: [The Lord] protects the strangers who live in our land;
he helps widows and orphans. . . .
P: Praise the Lord!
ALL: The Lord is king forever,
Your God, O Zion, will reign for all time.
Praise the Lord.

Prayers of Petition   (selected verses)

Individuals will have four or five minutes to skim the Psalms looking for one to three verses of one or more Psalms that express prayers of petition. The words of the Psalmist should be words with which the individuals can identify. After time for skimming and selecting verses, let those who wish to offer their Psalm prayers of petition do so.

Words of Promise and Hope (selected verses)

L: This God—how perfect are his deeds!
How dependable his words!
He is like a shield for all who seek his protection.
The Lord alone is God;
God alone is our defense.
                              Psalm 18:30-31

P: I wait patiently for God to save me;
I depend on him alone.
He alone protects and saves me;

45

he is my defender,
and I shall never be defeated.
I depend upon God alone;
I put my hope in him.

Psalm 62:1, 2, 5

L: God is our shelter and strength,
always ready to help in times of trouble.
So we will not be afraid, even if the earth is
shaken
and mountains fall into the ocean
depths . . .
Come and see what the Lord has done.
See what amazing things he has done on
earth.
He stops wars all over the world;
he breaks bows, destroys spears. . . .

Psalm 46:1, 2, 8, 9

P: I am listening to what the Lord God is saying;
he promises peace to us, his own people,
if we do not go back to our foolish ways.
Surely he is ready to save those who honor
him,
and his saving presence will remain in our
land.
Love and faithfulness will meet;
righteousness and peace will embrace.

Psalm 85:8-10

Psalms and the Gospel Message

(The people will read a Psalm passage, and
the leader will read a passage from the New
Testament that serves as an echo to the Psalm
passage.)

P: The Lord is my shepherd;
I have everything I need.

Psalm 23:1

L: [Jesus said,] "I am the Good Shepherd,
who is willing to die for the sheep."

John 10:11

P: God put a cloud over his people
and a fire at night to give them light.

Psalm 105:39

L: [Jesus said,] "I am the light of the world.
Whoever follows me will have the light of
life and will never walk in darkness."

John 8:12

P: [God] gave them food from heaven to
satisfy them.

He opened a rock, and water gushed out,
flowing through the desert like a river.

Psalm 105:40b-41

L: "I am the bread of life," Jesus told them.
"He who comes to me will never be hungry;
he who believes in me will never be thirsty."

John 6:35

P: The Lord has chosen Zion;
he wants to make it his home:
"This is where I will live forever;
this is were I want to rule.
I will richly provide Zion with all she needs;
I will satisfy her poor with food. . . .
Here I will make one of David's descendants a great king;
here I will preserve the rule of my chosen
king."

Psalm 132:13-15, 17a

L: Then I saw a new heaven and a new earth.
The first heaven and the first earth disappeared, and the sea vanished. And I saw the
Holy City, the new Jerusalem, coming
down out of heaven from God. . . . I heard
a loud voice speaking from the throne:
"Now God's home is with mankind! He will
live with them, and they shall be his people.
God himself will be with them, and he will
be their God. He will wipe away all tears
from their eyes. There will be no more
death, no more grief or crying in pain. The
old things have disappeared." . . . And now
I make all things new!"

Revelation 21:1-5

Prayer of Thanksgiving (Lined by the leader)
Psalm 145 (selected verses)

I will proclaim your greatness, my God and king;
I will thank you forever and ever.
Every day I will thank you;
I will praise you forever and ever. . . .
What you have done will be praised
from one generation to the next;
they will proclaim your mighty acts. . . .
They will tell about all your goodness
and sing about your kindness. . . .
All your creatures, Lord, will praise you,
and all your people will give you thanks. . . .
[Praise and thanks to thee, O God.]

Amen.

Benediction   (By the Leader)
                Psalm 27:14

Trust in the Lord.
   Have faith, do not despair.
Trust in the Lord.

PART TWO

Teaching the Psalms: Ten Activities

Protect me, O God;
  I trust in you for safety.
I say to the Lord, "You are my Lord;
  all the good things I have come from you." . . .
I am always aware of the Lord's presence;
  he is near and nothing can shake me.
And so I am thankful and glad,
  and I feel completely secure.

                                    Psalm 16:1-2, 8-9

Introduction

Teaching the Psalms can be a delightful experience for teachers because we have the opportunity to spend a lot of time with one of the most inspiring books of the Bible and because we can celebrate the new insights and inspiration that come to the participants as they experience the Psalms. Studying the Psalms can be a growing experience for the participants as they look carefully at various types of Psalms, as they work hard at interpreting the meanings of the Psalms, and as they relate their understandings of the Psalms to their own spiritual development. The variety of psalm types, the difficulty of interpreting many Psalms, and the relationship of Psalms to the worship experiences of most Christian churches and Jewish synagogues all provide sufficient reasons for spending a significant amount of time teaching and studying the Psalms.

In the ten teaching activities that follow, there are enough suggestions for as many as twenty-five one-hour study sessions. It is not expected that teachers will use all ten activities in the sequence presented with a class in one course of study. Ordinarily, it will be more effective to use these activities as a basis for planning a series of six to thirteen sessions. Teachers will want to consider the needs and interests of the participants—being realistic about the time available and assessing to what extent the participants will truly participate. Teachers will want also to be selective from among the ten activities, as well as adding and adapting in order to prepare for the number of scheduled sessions.

Surely the teachers will have done a lot of reading (and praying) of the Psalms as well as reading about the Psalms in order to prepare for teaching. This background information will be very helpful to the teachers. However, the ten activities as outlined are designed in such a way that teachers are expected to do a minimum of presenting information about the Psalms, and the students are expected to do a maximum of participating with and experiencing the Psalms directly. In these activities teachers are primarily guides, as they give directions and monitor the process of exploring and encountering the Psalms. The exceptions to this approach may be chapters 11 and 12 if teachers choose to present most of the information.

I present these ten activities with a logical sequence in mind. However, teachers who review the activities will notice that there are many ways to mix and match the activities and to rearrange their sequence. It is crucial to the teachers' satisfaction and success in teaching the Psalms that the given suggestions are added to, adapted, and rearranged—making the completed teaching plans truly a product of the teachers' own creativity. The participants will be much more motivated, as will the teachers, when they are engaged in a creative process rather than just following slavishly the plans someone else devised for a different group in another setting.

11

Introducing the Psalms

Setting the Stage

As we have already affirmed, the book of Psalms is a unique literary collection. It is a compilation of mixed types written and edited by those from many different historical settings for assorted purposes. It is often difficult for the casual reader of Psalms to distinguish all these

THE PSALMS ②

BOOK I ③

1 Blessed is the man
who walks not in the counsel of
the wicked,
nor stands in the way of sinners,
nor sits in the seat of scoffers;
2 but his delight is in the law of the
LORD,
and on his law he meditates day and
night.
3 He is like a tree
planted by streams of water,
that yields its fruit in its season,
and its leaf does not wither.
In all that he does, he prospers.

4 The wicked are not so,
but are like chaff which the wind
drives away.
5 Therefore the wicked will not stand in
the judgment,
nor sinners in the congregation of
the righteous;
6 for the LORD knows the way of the
righteous,
but the way of the wicked will
perish.

2 Why do the nations conspire,
and the peoples plot in vain?
2 The kings of the earth set themselves,
and the rulers take counsel together,
against the LORD and his anointed,
saying,
3 "Let us burst their bonds asunder,
and cast their cords from us."

4 He who sits in the heavens laughs;
the LORD has them in derision.
5 Then he will speak to them in his
wrath,
and terrify them in his fury, saying,
6 "I have set my king
on Zion, my holy hill."

7 I will tell of the decree of the LORD:
He said to me, "You are my son,
today I have begotten you.

8 Ask of me, and I will make the nations
your heritage,
and the ends of the earth your possession.
9 You shall break them with a rod of
iron,
and dash them in pieces like a
potter's vessel."

10 Now therefore, O kings, be wise;
be warned, O rulers of the earth. ⑦ᵃ
11 Serve the LORD with fear,
with trembling 12kiss his feet,ᵃ
lest he be angry, and you perish in
the way;
for his wrath is quickly kindled.

Blessed are all who take refuge in him.

④

A Psalm of David, when he fled from
Absalom his son. ⑤

3 O LORD, how many are my foes!
Many are rising against me;
2 many are saying of me,
there is no help for him in God.
Selah ⑥

3 But thou, O LORD, art a shield about
me,
my glory, and the lifter of my head.
4 I cry aloud to the LORD,
and he answers me from his holy
hill. Selah

5 I lie down and sleep;
I wake again, for the LORD sustains
me.
6 I am not afraid of ten thousands of
people
who have set themselves against me
round about.

7 Arise, O LORD!
Deliver me, O my God!
For thou dost smite all my enemies on
the cheek,
thou dost break the teeth of the
wicked.

⑦ᵇ ᵃ Cn: The Hebrew of 11b and 12a is uncertain
1.1-3: Jer 17.7-8. 2.1-2: Acts 4.25-26. 2.7: Mt 3.17; Acts 13.33; Heb 1.5; 5.5; 2 Pet 1.17. ⑦
2.8-9: Rev 2.26; 12.5; 19.15.

unique features of Psalms. When we have a little information about type, author, setting, structure, and purpose of the Psalms, then our understanding and appreciation are enhanced.

This activity is primarily in the form of presenting information. There are two worksheets that participants may use to follow along with the leader/teacher. If sufficient resources (Bible dictionaries, commentaries, etc.) are available so that each group member can use at least one resource, each participant can be assigned a different one of the twelve notations to work alone or in small groups to determine the significance of each notation.

What is presented in this activity can be expanded and spread over two or three sessions, depending upon how much detail the participants want to deal with and how much they want to do for themselves. Or, a part or two of the activity can be omitted depending upon the time available and the interests of the group. It is best not to rush parts of the activity because participants may become frustrated if they feel they are not comprehending the material quickly enough.

Ordinarily this activity will provide the basis for one or more introductory sessions in a course of study. It is important to begin work at a comfortable pace in order for the participants to become motivated and involved with the process so that they will be ready and eager to experience further activities.

In order to be fully prepared and somewhat knowledgeable of the several topics in this activity, the leader/teacher will find it helpful to read the introduction to a commentary on Psalms and an article in a Bible dictionary or another book that provides an overview of the Psalms. There are a number of helpful resources described in the bibliography.

Opening Words

The Psalms are a very special anthology of prayers, hymns, poems, and liturgies. Many of our hymns find their origins in the Psalms. Psalms are memorized by the young. Psalms are read at the bedside of the ill and aged. Psalms are included in Sunday morning worship services, as well as in special services such as funerals. Many people, young and old, find the Psalms to be a source of strength and comfort in their own spiritual pilgrimages. Dietrich Bonhoeffer referred to the book of Psalms as "the prayerbook of the Bible," and one of the last things he wrote from prison was a tract by that title (see bibliography). In order to understand and appreciate the Psalms more, it will be helpful for us to spend some time exploring some of their special features.

Look at a Psalm

Let us look at the first page of the whole book of Psalms and specifically at Psalms 1 to 3. Page one of the Revised Standard Version translation of the Bible precedes. Notice that there are seven notations. Each of these notations refers to an important feature of the book of Psalms.

1. The Page Number

Obviously the page number itself is not significant, but it does represent the placement of the book of Psalms in the canon. Page 464 is the last page of the book of Job and 547 is the first page of the book of Proverbs.

These two books, with Psalms and other books such as Ecclesiastes, Song of Solomon, and Lamentations, form the third major portion of the canon identified as Writings or Wisdom Literature. These books are believed to be products of the Post-Exilic period and were accepted as sacred scripture by the time of Jesus. Psalms is not only the largest of these books but is also the most remembered, quoted, and used of the books of wisdom.

2. The Psalms—Title of the Book

The Hebrew title of the book is "Tehillim," which means "songs of praise." Tehillim is formed from the same root (h-l-l) as the word hallelujah. The English title, Psalms, finds its origin in the Greek word psalmos, which is a translation of the Hebrew word mismor used as a preface to 57 of the Psalms (see the preface or title to Psalm 3, written as "A Psalm of David . . ."). The Greek word psalmos means a song sung to the accompaniment of stringed instruments.

In the New Testament, there are several

specific references to Psalms *(psalmos):* "For David himself says in the book of Psalms . . ." (Luke 20:42); "Everything written about me in the Law of Moses, the writings of the prophets, and the Psalms had to come true" (Luke 24:44); "For it is written in the book of Psalms . . ." (Acts 1:20); "As it is written in the second Psalm . . ." (Acts 13:33); "Speak to one another with the words of psalms, hymns . . . sing hymns and psalms to the Lord with praise in your hearts" (Ephesians 5:19); and "Teach and instruct one another with all wisdom. Sing psalms, hymns, and sacred songs; sing to God with thanksgiving in your hearts" (Colossians 3:16).

3. Book I

The book of Psalms is composed of five sections that are specifically identified as Book I, Book II, etc. There is no clear rationale for the division of the Psalms into five books that are: Psalms 1-41; 42-72; 73-89, 90-106, and 107-150. They are not equal in length, and there is no common theme, author, or characteristic for the Psalms of a given book. Tradition suggests that the number five is associated with the books of the Pentateuch (Genesis, Exodus, Leviticus, Numbers, and Deuteronomy), commonly identified as the Books of Moses, the Law. The Pentateuch is attributed to Moses, as the Psalms are attributed to David, and there are five books in each.

One characteristic of each of the five books of Psalms is that the last verse of each book is in the form of a doxology, as in "Praise the Lord, the God of Israel! Praise him now and forever! Amen! Amen!" The exact words are a little different in each ending doxology (Psalms 41:13, 72:19, 89:52, 106:48, and 150:6) but each is clearly an affirmation of praise with the words, "Praise the Lord." The whole of Psalm 150 is a doxology of praise, which serves not only as an ending for Book V but also as an ending to the whole book of the Psalms.

When and why the Psalms were organized into five separate sections or books is unknown.

4. "A Psalm of David . . ."

Approximately two-thirds of the Psalms have headings or titles that attribute the Psalms to one or another person or groups of persons. The names included in one or more headings and the Psalms so designated are:

a. *of David,* seventy-two times (Psalms 3-9, 11-32, 34-41, 51-65, 68-70, 86, 103, 108-110, 122, 124, 131, and 138-145). The reference is to King David but also denotes any king of the house of David. Whether or not David was the actual author is not as important as the fact that the compilers of the collection of Psalms recognized as many as seventy-two Psalms to reflect the life situation of David, the great king of Israel. Almost one-half of the Psalms bear the mark of David, whereas we commonly associate all of the Psalms with David.

b. *"of the sons of Korah,"* twelve times (Psalms 42, 44-49, 84-85, and 87-88). The likely reference is to a family of Levite priests, a guild of Temple singers.

c. *"of Asaph,"* twelve times (Psalms 50 and 73-83). The title is probably an abbreviation for "The sons of Asaph." According to I Chronicles 25:1-2, Asaph was a contemporary of David, one of the three families or guilds of Temple musicians charged with the overseeing of music, songs, and instruments for worship in the Temple.

d. *"of Solomon,"* (Psalms 72 and 127).

e. *"of Ethan the Ezrahite,"* (Psalm 89).

f. *"of Moses,"* (Psalm 90). It is not likely that Moses is the actual author of the Psalm, but tradition may have attributed it to him because the content can be identified with the time of Moses.

5. "When he [David] fled from Absalom his son."

Sixteen of the Psalms have, as part of the heading or in the first verse, a specific historical context. It is quite possible that those compiling the Psalms at a later time, after returning from exile, quite intentionally connected the message of the particular Psalms with remembered events in the history of their people. There are many other Psalms that can be related to historical periods or events as a result of interpreting key words or passages. See for example, Psalm 42, which gives some clues that the author is one in exile.

6. Selah

This word, *Selah,* in the right margin appears seventy-one times in thirty-nine different Psalms. Even though the term appears often, its interpretation remains varied. Many biblical scholars propose that *Selah* provides some sort of musical or liturgical cue for singers and musicians. Here are several possible definitions:

a. One possibility is that it is a cue for an interlude during which something else was either sung or played.
b. Another possibility is that the word is derived from a Hebrew root (s-l-l), which means "to lift up." "To lift up" may suggest lifting up one's voice to sing louder or lifting up the sound of the music—to play or sing louder.
c. A third option is that the word is based upon an Aramaic root (s-l-h), which means "to turn, to bend, or to pray." This may have been a cue for the worshipers to kneel, to bow, or to fall prostrate in humble, respectful submission to God.

One cannot be sure which interpretation is most accurate. I consider all three as possibilities and see each one as an appropriate response by worshipers, as they pray together these thirty-nine Psalms.

7. Footnotes

On almost every page of Psalms in many Bibles, there are footnotes. These footnotes are often helpful for interpreting particular words or passages. On the sample page reprinted in this activity, there are two kinds of footnotes:

a. When you read Psalm 2:11-12 you will notice a lower case "a" that directs you to the bottom of the page where the "a" reappears followed by "Cn: The Hebrew of 11*b* and 12*a* is uncertain." You must turn to the preface of the Bible to find the meanings of abbreviations such as "Cn," and you discover "Cn" indicates that a correction was made where the text has suffered in transmission" and "none of the versions provides a satisfactory restoration"; the translation committee agrees with the "best judgment of competent

scholars as to the most probable reconstruction of the original text."
b. The second type of footnote provides cross-references between the Psalm passages and other passages in the Bible. You will notice in boldface type the numbers 1:1-3, referring to Psalm 1, verses 1-3. Following is the reference to "Jer. 17:7-8," which means that in the book of Jeremiah, chapter 17, verses 7-8, you will find the essence of Psalm 1:1-3 repeated.

Look at Two More Psalms

We have looked at seven different references for page one; let us now look at two other Psalms that provide some additional clues to reading and understanding the Psalms. (See page 56.)

8. "To the choirmaster":

This phrase is found in the headings of fifty-five Psalms. It has also been translated as "to the director" and "to the chief musician." The meaning of the Hebrew is uncertain. However, this phrase does suggest that such Psalms were intended to be used in corporate worship experiences.

9. "According to Do Not Destroy"

In addition to Psalm 57, three other Psalms include this citation in the heading (Psalms 58, 59, and 75). Again the Hebrew word is not known. It is possible that the term refers to some ritual act, a mode of singing, or a secular tune. There are several similar citations in other Psalms: "according to Lilies" (Psalms 45, 69, and 80); "according to The Gittith" (Psalms 8, 81, and 84); "according to Alamoth" (Psalm 46); and "according to The Dove on Far-off Terebinths" (Psalm 56). The meaning of all of these is uncertain in the Hebrew.

10. "A Miktam of David"

We have already discussed the question of Psalms being attributed to David. In this Psalm the word *Miktam* means a "psalm of atone-

To the choirmaster: according to Do Not Destroy. A Miktam of David, when he fled from Saul, in the cave.

57 Be merciful to me, O God,
   be merciful to me,
      for in thee my soul takes refuge;
   in the shadow of thy wings I will
      take refuge,
      till the storms of destruction pass
      by.
2 I cry to God Most High,
   to God who fulfils his purpose for
      me.
3 He will send from heaven and save
      me,
   he will put to shame those who
      trample upon me. *Selah*
   God will send forth his steadfast
      love and his faithfulness!

4 I lie in the midst of lions
   that greedily devour⁴ the sons of
      men;
   their teeth are spears and arrows,
      their tongues sharp swords.

5 Be exalted, O God, above the
      heavens!
   Let thy glory be over all the earth!

6 They set a net for my steps;
   my soul was bowed down.
   They dug a pit in my way,
      but they have fallen into it them-
      selves. *Selah*

7 My heart is steadfast, O God,
   my heart is steadfast!
   I will sing and make melody!
8   Awake, my soul!
   Awake, O harp and lyre!
   I will awake the dawn!
9 I will give thanks to thee, O Lord,
   among the peoples;

   I will sing praises to thee among
      the nations.
10 For thy steadfast love is great to the
      heavens,
   thy faithfulness to the clouds.

11 Be exalted, O God, above the
      heavens!
   Let thy glory be over all the
      earth!

To the choirmaster: with stringed instruments. A Psalm. A Song.

67 May God be gracious to us
   and bless us
   and make his face to shine upon
      us, *Selah*
2 that thy way may be known upon
      earth,
   thy saving power among all na-
      tions.

3 Let the peoples praise thee, O God;
   let all the peoples praise thee!

4 Let the nations be glad and sing for
      joy,
   for thou dost judge the peoples
      with equity
   and guide the nations upon earth.
      Selah
5 Let the peoples praise thee, O God;
   let all the peoples praise thee!

6 The earth has yielded its increase;
   God, our God, has blessed us.
7 God has blessed us;
   let all the ends of the earth fear
      him!

ment." The word appears in the headings of six Psalms (Psalm 16, 56-60).

11. "With stringed instruments"

Again we have a note as to how the Psalm is to be presented in the context of corporate worship. "With stringed instruments" possibly suggests that some other instruments usually accompanying singing, such as percussion or wind instruments, would be excluded in the accompaniment to this Psalm, plus Psalms 4, 6, 54, 55, 61, and 76 where the direction also appears. It seems that the use of "with stringed instruments" in this Psalm is redundant since the technical meaning of the word *Psalm* is a song sung to the accompaniment of stringed instruments.

12. "A Psalm. A Song"

The word *Psalm* appears in the headings of fifty-seven Psalms, and as previously stated, above the word is a Greek translation *(psalmos)* of the Hebrew *(mizmor),* which means "a song sung to the accompaniment of stringed instruments." The Hebrew word for *song* is a common term for secular as well as religious songs and is found in the headings of some thirty Psalms.

The Structure of Psalms

The Psalms are written, and therefore printed, in the form of poetry. Even without the designation of verse numbers, it is clear where the beginnings and endings are for most of the lines. For the Psalmist it was not necessary for one line to rhyme with the next; rather it was important to match the thoughts or concepts of one line with the next. We will look at Psalms 27 and 103 in order to gain a sense of the poetic structure of Psalms. (See page 58.)

Notice that ordinarily there are two or three parts for each verse. These parts are often called stich (stik) from a Greek word *stichos* meaning "row, line, or verse." Each stich or line repeats, complements, or completes the thought of the verse. In Hebrew poetry each verse presents a complete idea or concept.

Look at Psalm 27. Read each verse separately. Notice that all the stichs of each verse are related to the same concept and present a complete thought.

As we read Psalm 27, look to see how many verses have two stichs and how many have three or more. Also, observe an exception in verse nine. The number "nine" is associated with the wrong line if it is to designate the beginning of a new thought. Actually the line that begins verse nine, "Don't hide yourself from me," completes the thought of verse eight. The number "nine" should begin the next stich, "Don't be angry with me."

Now look at Psalm 103, and continue reading each verse to see how many stichs are in each one and notice what the complete thought of each is.

Look again at Psalms 27 and 103. There are spaces between some of the verses, such as between 27:6 and 27:7 and between 103:5 and 103:6. Each space indicates the separation between one stanza or strophe and another. Each strophe is composed of two to eight or more verses. The break between one strophe and another is usually determined by a change in theme, change in mood, change in who is speaking or to whom it is addressed, or because of some other emphasis. By counting the strophes in Psalm 27, we notice there are seven of them, and in Psalm 103 there are four strophes. Spend a few minutes looking closely at these two Psalms. Read each strophe carefully and after determining the emphasis for a strophe, give it a title. Do this for Psalms 27 and 103 or some other Psalms—perhaps a favorite.

There are four different forms of poetic parallelism that appear most frequently in the Psalms: synonymous, synthetic, antithetic, and comparative.

In *synonymous parallelism* the two parts or stichs of a verse repeat the same thought in different words. Something new may be added in the second stich but this line is essentially a reinforcement of the thought of the first stich.

Praise the Lord, my soul!
   All my being, praise his holy name! (103:1).

He does not keep on rebuking;
   he is not angry forever (103:9).

I have asked the Lord for one thing;
   one thing only do I want (27:4).

A Prayer of Praise'

27 The LORD is my light and my salvation;
    I will fear no one.
The LORD protects me from all danger;
    I will never be afraid.

2 When evil men attack me and try to kill me,
    they stumble and fall.
3 Even if a whole army surrounds me,
    I will not be afraid;
even if enemies attack me,
    I will still trust God.⁵

4 I have asked the LORD for one thing;
    one thing only do I want:
to live in the LORD's house all my life,
    to marvel there at his goodness,
    and to ask for his guidance.
5 In times of trouble he will shelter me;
    he will keep me safe in his Temple
    and make me secure on a high rock.
6 So I will triumph over my enemies around me.
    With shouts of joy I will offer sacrifices in his Temple;
    I will sing, I will praise the LORD.

7 Hear me, LORD, when I call to you!
    Be merciful and answer me!
8 When you said, "Come worship me,"
    I answered, "I will come, LORD."
9   Don't hide yourself from me!

Don't be angry with me;
    don't turn your servant away.
You have been my help;
    don't leave me, don't abandon me,
    O God, my savior.
10 My father and mother may abandon me,
    but the LORD will take care of me.

11 Teach me, LORD, what you want me to do,
    and lead me along a safe path,
    because I have many enemies.
12 Don't abandon me to my enemies,
    who attack me with lies and threats.

13 I know that I will live to see
    the LORD's goodness in this present life.
14 Trust in the LORD.
    Have faith, do not despair.
    Trust in the LORD.

— Verse

Stich 1
Stich 2
Stich 3
Stich 4
Stich 5

= One verse

Strophe or stanza

Stichs (or lines)

The Love of God

103 Praise the LORD, my soul!
    All my being, praise his holy name!
2 Praise the LORD, my soul,
    and do not forget how kind he is.
3 He forgives all my sins
    and heals all my diseases.
4 He keeps me from the grave
    and blesses me with love and mercy.
5 He fills my life with good things,
    so that I stay young and strong like an eagle.

6 The LORD judges in favor of the oppressed
    and gives them their rights.
7 He revealed his plans to Moses
    and let the people of Israel see his mighty deeds.
8 The LORD is merciful and loving,
    slow to become angry and full of constant love.
9 He does not keep on rebuking;
    he is not angry forever.
10 He does not punish us as we deserve
    or repay us for our sins and wrongs.
11 As high as the sky is above the earth,
    so great is his love for those who have reverence for him.
12 As far as the east is from the west,
    so far does he remove our sins from us.
13 As kind as a father is to his children,
    so kind is the LORD to those who honor him.
14 He knows what we are made of;
    he remembers that we are dust.

15 As for us, our life is like grass.
    We grow and flourish like a wild flower;
16   then the wind blows on it, and it is gone—
    no one sees it again.
17 But for those who honor the LORD, his love lasts forever,
    and his goodness endures for all generations
18 of those who are true to his covenant
    and who faithfully obey his commands.

19 The LORD placed his throne in heaven;
    he is king over all.
20 Praise the LORD, you strong and mighty angels,
    who obey his commands,
    who listen to what he says.
21 Praise the LORD, all you heavenly powers,
    you servants of his, who do his will!
22 Praise the LORD, all his creatures
    in all the places he rules.
    Praise the LORD, my soul!

In *synthetic parallelism* something new is added to the thought of the first stich by adding it to the second stich. Think of it as a "stair-step" approach where one moves from one concept (step) to another concept (step).

He forgives all my sins
and heals all my diseases (103:3).

When you said, "Come worship me,"
I answered, "I will come, Lord" (27:8).

In *antithetic parallelism* the second stich expresses just the opposite thought of the first stich. It is not a matter of saying one thing differently but rather of making two different, opposing points.

My father and mother may abandon me,
but the Lord will take care of me (27:10).

In *comparative parallelism* the second stich expresses a thought in comparison to the first stich. These stiches can be thought of as "baby parables." They are somewhat like synonymous parallelism except that instead of repeating the thought in different words, there is the element of metaphor, using "picture words" in one stich to explain the thought of the other stich.

As high as the sky is above the earth,
so great is his love for those who have reverence for him (103:11).

As kind as a father is to his children,
so kind is the Lord to those who honor him (103:13).

One other type of poetry we must consider before moving on is the acrostic poem. An acrostic is where the first or last letter of a series of words, lines, or verses spells out something. We encounter acrostics in many places. T.G.I.F. is familiar to many as **T**hank **G**od **I**t's **F**riday, and in some places in the country T.G.I. Friday's is a favorite restaurant. Children learn the alphabet as an acrostic when they associate A for apple, B for ball, C for cat, and on through the alphabet. There are nine Psalms that are constructed as acrostic poems where each of the twenty-two letters of the Hebrew alphabet is used in sequence to begin either each stich (Psalms 111 and 112), each verse (Psalms 25, 34, and 145),

pair of verses (Psalms 9, 10, and 37), or strophe (Psalm 119). To illustrate what I mean, the following excerpts from four different Psalms are printed on page 60, from *The Book of Psalms: A New Translation According to the Traditional Hebrew Text,* published by the Jewish Publication Society of America. (I commend this wonderful translation to anyone who desires to read the Psalms in a fresh, new way.)

Reflecting on the Process

There is a lot of information in the preceding pages of this activity. It may be too much for one session for some groups. There are several ways that leaders/teachers can approach this content.

1. Be selective and share only some of the information in an introductory session. Then share more information in other sessions when it is appropriate or when asked.

2. Share some of the information in each of three or four other sessions, along with selected activities that are outlined on succeeding pages.

3. Encourage participants to do some homework by reading a resource book and selected Psalms so that they will learn the introductory content on their own. This will leave time in the class session for questions, answers, and sharing of information.

4. Use the worksheets provided for homework or for guiding participation during class time.

5. An efficient way, though not as effective, is for the leader to present the information in a lecture format using illustrations, handouts, or transparencies to facilitate the presentation.

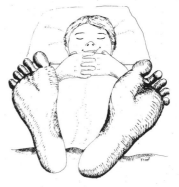

When I lie down, I go to sleep in peace;
you alone, O Lord, keep me perfectly safe.
Psalm 4:8

34 [A psalm] of David,
    [a]when he feigned madness in the presence of Abimelech,
    who turned him out, and he left.[a]   [a-a] Cf. I Sam. 21. 14

א 2 I bless the LORD at all times;
    praise of Him is ever in my mouth.
ב 3 I glory in the LORD;
    let the lowly hear it and rejoice.
ג 4 Exalt the LORD with me;
    let us extol His name together.
ד 5 I turned to the LORD, and He answered me;
    He saved me from all my terrors.

37 [A psalm] of David.

א   Do not be vexed by evil men;
        do not be incensed by wrongdoers;
    2   for they soon wither like grass,
        like verdure fade away.
ב 3 Trust in the LORD and do good,
        abide in the land and remain loyal.
    4 Urge your plea on the LORD,
        and He will grant you the desires of your heart.
ג 5 Leave all[a] to the LORD;   [a] Lit. "your way"
        trust in Him; He will do it.
    6 He will cause your vindication to shine forth like the light,
        the justice of your case, like the noonday sun.

112 Hallelujah.
א   Happy is the man who fears the LORD,
ב   who is greatly devoted to His commandments.
ג 2 His descendants will be mighty in the land,
ד   a blessed generation of upright men.
ה 3 Wealth and riches are in his house,
ו   and his beneficence lasts forever.
ז 4 [a]A light shines[a] for the upright in the darkness;
ח   he is gracious, compassionate and beneficent.
ט 5 All goes well with the man who lends generously,
י   who conducts his affairs with equity.

        [a-a] Or "He shines as a light"

119 Happy are those whose way is blameless,
א   who follow the teaching of the LORD.
    2 Happy are those who observe His decrees,
        who turn to Him wholeheartedly.
    3 They have done no wrong,
        but have followed His ways.
    4 You have commanded that Your precepts
        be kept diligently.
    5 Would that my ways were firm
        in keeping Your laws;
    6   then I would not be ashamed
        when I regard all Your commandments.
    7 I will praise You with a sincere heart
        as I learn Your just rules.
    8 I will keep Your laws;
        do not utterly forsake me.

    9 How can a young man keep his way pure?—
        by holding to Your word.
    10 I have turned to You with all my heart;
        do not let me stray from Your commandments.

A portion of the first page from the Psalms in the RSV Bible is reproduced below. Notice the seven different notations. Each notation refers to an important feature of the book of Psalms. Use available resources and work with one or more of the notations and related questions to see what information you can find.

1. What book precedes Psalms? What book follows Psalms? What is the significance of the placement of Psalms in the Old Testament?

2. What is the origin of the book's title?

3. What is the significance of "Book I"?

4. Are all the Psalms, "Psalms of David"? If not, who are the other authors?

5. What is the significance of this line, "When he fled from Absalom his son"? Do other Psalms have similar notations?

6. What does *Selah* mean?

7. Of what value are footnotes and cross-references?

THE PSALMS ②

BOOK I ③

1
Blessed is the man
  who walks not in the counsel of the wicked,
nor stands in the way of sinners,
  nor sits in the seat of scoffers;
² but his delight is in the law of the LORD,
  and on his law he meditates day and night.
³ He is like a tree
  planted by streams of water,
that yields its fruit in its season,
  and its leaf does not wither.
In all that he does, he prospers.

⁴ The wicked are not so,
  but are like chaff which the wind drives away.
⁵ Therefore the wicked will not stand in the judgment,
  nor sinners in the congregation of the righteous;
⁶ for the LORD knows the way of the righteous,
  but the way of the wicked will perish.

2 Why do the nations conspire, and the peoples plot in vain?
² The kings of the earth set themselves.

He said to me, "You are my son, today I have begotten you.
⁸ Ask of me, and I will make the nations your heritage,
  and the ends of the earth your possession.
⁹ You shall break them with a rod of iron,
  and dash them in pieces like a potter's vessel."

¹⁰ Now therefore, O kings, be wise;
  be warned, O rulers of the earth.
¹¹ Serve the LORD with fear,
  with trembling ¹² kiss his feet,ᵃ
lest he be angry, and you perish in the way;
  for his wrath is quickly kindled.

Blessed are all who take refuge in him.

A Psalm of David, when he fled from Ab'sa·lom his son. ④ ⑤

3 O LORD, how many are my foes!
  Many are rising against me;
² many are saying of me,
  there is no help for him in God. ⑥
  Selah

³ But thou, O LORD, art a shield about me,

ᵃ Cn: The Hebrew of 11b and 12a is uncertain
1.1-3: Jer 17.7-8. 2.1-2: Acts 4.25-26. 2.7: Mt 3.17; Acts 13.33; Heb 1.5; 5.5; 2 Pet 1.17.
2.8-9: Rev 2.26; 12.5; 19.15.

475 ① ⑦

Notice several notations (numbers 8 through 12) on the text from Psalms 57 and 67. These notations indicate important features of the book of Psalms. Use available resources and work with one or more of the notations and related questions to see what information you can find.

8. What is "the choirmaster"?

9. What does "according to Do Not Destroy" represent?

10. What does the phrase "a Miktam of David" mean?

11. Why would someone say that "with stringed instruments" is redundant?

12. How often does "A Song" appear in Psalms?

(9) (8) To the choirmaster: according to Do Not Destroy. A Miktam of David, when he fled from Saul, in the cave. (10)

57 Be merciful to me, O God,
    be merciful to me,
  for in thee my soul takes refuge;
  in the shadow of thy wings I will
    take refuge,
  till the storms of destruction pass
    by.
8 I cry to God Most High,
  to God who fulfils his purpose for
    me.
3 He will send from heaven and save
    me,
  he will put to shame those who
    trample upon me.   Selah
God will send forth his steadfast
  love and his faithfulness!

4 I lie in the midst of lions
  that greedily devour the sons of
    men;
  their teeth are spears and arrows,
    their tongues sharp swords.

5 Be exalted, O God, above the
    heavens!
  Let thy glory be over all the earth!

6 They set a net for my steps;
    my soul was bowed down.
  They dug a pit in my way,
    but they have fallen into it them-
      selves.   Selah

7 My heart is steadfast, O God,
    my heart is steadfast!
  I will sing and make melody!
8   Awake, my soul!
  Awake, O harp and lyre!
    I will awake the dawn!
9 I will give thanks to thee, O Lord,
    among the peoples;
  I will sing praises to thee among
    the nations.
10 For thy steadfast love is great to the
    heavens,
  thy faithfulness to the clouds.

11 Be exalted, O God, above the
    heavens!
  Let thy glory be over all the
    earth!

To the choirmaster: with stringed (11)
instruments. A Psalm. A Song. (12)

67 May God be gracious to us
    and bless us
  and make his face to shine upon
    us,   Selah
2 that thy way may be known upon
    earth,
  thy saving power among all na-
    tions.

3 Let the peoples praise thee, O God;
    let all the peoples praise thee!

4 Let the nations be glad and sing for
    joy,
  for thou dost judge the peoples
    with equity
  and guide the nations upon earth.
      Selah
5 Let the peoples praise thee, O God;
    let all the peoples praise thee!

6 The earth has yielded its increase;
    God, our God, has blessed us.
7 God has blessed us;
    let all the ends of the earth fear
      him!

12

Types of Psalms

Setting the Stage

Ever since the pioneering work of German scholar Hermann Gunkel (1862-1932), students of the Bible have been working with the Psalms not as a single literary piece but as a collection of Psalms that includes a variety of types. The Psalms originate from many historical settings. Some Psalms reflect personal life experiences and other Psalms seem to encompass a national, corporate situation. Some Psalms are truly prayers to God, and other Psalms are more didactic in presenting concepts about God.

As we read and pray the Psalms, we will do so with more understanding and appreciation when we can relate to individual Psalms that represent particular types. When a Psalm is identified by type and dealt with accordingly, there are built-in clues that assist in the interpretation and application of the Psalm.

In attempting to determine which psalm types to include in this activity, I was interested to learn there is no consensus among biblical scholars as to the number of types. On the one hand there is the suggestion that most of the Psalms can be identified as either a cry of lament or a hymn of praise (Westermann). In a sense, that is true because these are the two dominant emotions that characterize Psalms. These two types are further subdivided by others, so that types such as the following are described: individual laments, community laments, songs of thanksgiving, hymns of praise, liturgies, holy history, and wisdom Psalms. I have discovered that the more types we can describe, the more helpful students will find this teaching activity. I have developed descriptions for twelve different types of psalms, which is more than is described in most of the commentaries and monographs on Psalms. However, for teaching/learning purposes I have found more comprehension and involvement on the part of the participants when there are this many types to work with.

There are several guidelines that participants must be aware of as they work with the various types of psalms:

1. Not all Psalms can be classified neatly into one type or another. There are often elements of two or more types in one Psalm. However, usually there is a dominant theme or characteristic expression.
2. Sometimes the designation of a Psalm as one type or another seems to be arbitrary. It is important for the participant to realize that naming and placing Psalms into types is very much a human endeavor and is subject to refinement and revision as well as personal judgment.
3. The elements used to identify a particular type are not always found in the same sequence in all the Psalms, nor are all the elements always present.
4. When working with psalm types, it is important for the readers/participants to try to understand why the authors/teachers have classified particular Psalms in the way they have. It is equally important for the readers/participants to feel free to name and describe their own categories and to so designate particular Psalms as they understand them.

In this teaching activity the twelve psalm types are presented with brief descriptions and an example from several verses of a representative Psalm to illustrate each type. Six or more of the psalm types are developed with more thoroughness in the seven teaching activities that follow this one. Ordinarily it would be best to use this activity prior to using any of the other six but the teachers/leaders may find that a particular group will be ready to work with a specific psalm type without doing this activity first.

Leading the Activity

Leaders/teachers can use any of the content presented in the "Setting the Stage" section as an introduction to this activity. It is helpful to read a portion of a commentary or monograph on Psalms that deals with the matter of psalm types as preparation for guiding others in this activity.

A Matching Exercise

Without giving any specific examples of the various psalm types, it is challenging for participants to try to complete the matching exercise on page 65. The chosen lines are explicitly representative of a particular type. There are no trick items intended. This exercise should not be presented as a test, but rather as a way for one to start discriminating between one type of psalm and another. Provide about ten minutes to complete the exercise.

Compare Responses

After participants have completed the matching exercise, encourage them to work in pairs to compare their responses. Because of the limited evidence on which to make a judgment (verses rather than complete Psalms), limited time, and limited knowledge about psalm types, neither the participants nor the leader should expect a large number of correct matchings of type to sample verse. However, it will be helpful for individuals to compare their judgments with one another. Comparing notes and giving the reasons for their choices will help persons begin to look for key words that distinguish one type from another. After a brief period of comparing notes, the leader should give the correct answers. (Remember that there may be legitimate differences of opinion, so the "correct" answers may be challenged for good reason. Be ready for that possibility.)

Features of Psalm Types

Now that everyone has begun to think about key words and features that distinguish one psalm type from another, it is time to make a brief presentation describing each type. Be sure to remind the participants that there will be other teaching activities that deal in more detail with some of the types.

What follows could become a lengthy presentation. The important thing to keep in mind is that most of the psalm types will be worked with again in other activities. To assist in the presentation, do either or both of two things:

1. Prepare a worksheet with the titles of the twelve psalm types, leaving space between each for participants to write a few notes. Also, it is helpful to have a transparency with the twelve titles in the order that they will be presented.

2. Prepare several pages that have copies of twelve different Psalms so that there is a good example of each type. Participants can refer to their own Bibles if copies aren't available.

Descriptions of Psalm Types

1. Psalms of Praise and Thanksgiving

There are quite a few Psalms that fit this category (approximately thirty). Usually the Psalm begins by either addressing God, or the audience, with an acknowledgement of God's presence. Key words are: *praise, give thanks, glory, sing, joy,* and *joyful.*

The opening of the Psalm is often followed by a longer portion where the reasons for the praise and thanksgiving are outlined. The reasons given may be God's action in creation, God's saving acts in Israel's history, God's holiness and authority, or God's covenant relationship with the people.

Sometimes there is an ending to the Psalm that reaffirms the Psalmist's call or intention to praise God. Other times the Psalm just concludes by stating why God is worthy of praise.

A familiar, classic example of the Psalms of praise and thanksgiving is Psalm 100:

Sing to the Lord, all the world!
Worship the Lord with Joy;
   come before him with happy songs!
Acknowledge that the Lord is God.
   He made us and we belong to him;
   we are his people, we are his flock.

Enter the Temple gates with thanksgiving;
   go into its courts with praise.

Matching Exercise

Read the lines from Psalms in the left column. Look for the name of a psalm type in the right column that matches the quote. Place the appropriate number* in the blank. Take ten minutes to complete this activity.

Words from Representative Psalms	*Psalm Type*

1. "The Lord is great and is to be highly praised in the city of our God, on his sacred hill" (Ps. 48:1).

2. "You have rejected us, God, and defeated us; you have been angry with us—" (Ps. 60:1).

3. "The king is glad, O Lord, because you gave him strength; he rejoices because you made him victorious" (Ps. 21:1).

4. "Teach me, Lord, the meaning of your laws, and I will obey them at all times" (Ps. 119:33).

5. "Sing a new song to him, play the harp with skill, and shout for joy!" (Ps. 33:3).

6. "I wait patiently for God to save me; I depend on him alone" (Ps. 62:1).

7. "Light shines in the darkness for good men, for those who are merciful, kind, and just" (Ps. 112:4).

8. "He [the Lord] sits on his throne . . . and the earth shakes" (Ps. 99:1).

9. "You have set the earth firmly on its foundations, and it will never be moved" (Ps. 104:5).

10. "Let the people of Israel say, 'His love is eternal.' Let the priests of God say, 'His love is eternal.' Let all who worship him say, 'His love is eternal'" (Ps. 118:2-4).

11. "My God, my God, why have you abandoned me?" (Ps. 22:1).

12. "Our ancestors in Egypt did not understand God's wonderful acts; they forgot the many times he showed them his love" (Ps. 106:7).

Psalm Type:

(5) Psalms of Praise and Thanksgiving

(9) Creation Psalms

(12) Salvation History Psalms

(8) Psalms of the Lord as King

(1) Hymns of Zion (Praise of Jerusalem)

(3) Royal Psalms (the King of Israel)

(11) Individual Psalms of Lament

(2) Community Psalms of Lament

(6) Psalms of Trust

(4) Torah Psalms

(7) Wisdom Psalms

(10) Liturgical Psalms

*The correct numbers are included here. When preparing the worksheet be sure to omit the numbers.

Give thanks to him and praise him.
The Lord is good;
    his love is eternal
    and his faithfulness lasts forever.

Other examples of Psalms of praise and thanksgiving include: 9, 27, 29, 30, 65, 66, 67, 92, 100, 103, 113, 116, 133, and 145-150.

2. Creation Psalms

This type could be included with the Psalms of praise and thanksgiving because they are Psalms praising God the creator. There are many Psalms where there is a line or two that refers to God the creator. Two examples are:

Come, let us bow down and worship him;
    let us kneel before the Lord, our Maker!
                                        Psalm 95:6

By his wisdom he made the heavens;
    his love is eternal;
he built the earth on the deep waters;
    his love is eternal.
He made the sun and the moon;
    his love is eternal.
                                        Psalm 136:5-7

As we read the Psalms, we will find many references to God the creator. As we look for Psalms where the whole Psalm focuses on God the creator, we notice that there are four: Psalms 8, 19:1-6, 104, and 148. Psalm 8 responds to two questions: (1) who is God? and (2) who is the human being? It is a brief hymn that celebrates the glory of God and the honored place of humankind in relation to God.

Psalm 19:1-6 is very clearly a hymn proclaiming God to be creator and is quite distinct from verses 7-14 that focus on the law of the Lord. In a sense we have two distinct Psalms. Psalm 19:1-6 declares what God has done in creating day and night with the sun to rule the day. There is no allusion to the human being in this Psalm.

Psalm 104 also praises God as creator of the heavens, the earth, all living creatures, moon, sun, and sea, and as the one who preserves all that has been created. It is interesting to compare the order of creation in this Psalm with the order as presented in Genesis 1.

Psalm 148 is a hymn of praise to God the creator. In addition to mention of the heavens, the earth, sun, moon, and all living creatures, there is mention of "kings and all peoples . . . girls and young men, old people and children too" (11, 12).

In the creation Psalms, we are led to worship the creator rather than to worship the results of God's creation. The Psalmist reminds us that as we sit at the lakeside in awe of the beauty of the sunrise or the sunset, it is the creator of the sun to whom we sing our praises. To worship the sun would be to worship a god other than the one proclaimed by the Psalmist.

3. Salvation History Psalms

There are many Psalms that have brief reference to God's mighty acts on behalf of his chosen people. In Psalms of praise, lament, and trust there are references over and over again to God's great deeds of redeeming the righteous from death, from enemies, from sin, and from defeat. Two examples of lines in Psalms that call attention to God's saving acts are:

You brought a grapevine out of Egypt;
    you drove out other nations and planted it
        in their land.
You cleared a place for it to grow;
    its roots went deep, and it spread out over
        the whole land.
                                        Psalm 80:8-9

With our own ears we have heard it, O God—
    our ancestors have told us about it,
    about the great things you did in their time,
    in the days of long ago:
how you yourself drove out the heathen
    and established your people in their land.
                                        Psalm 44:1-2

There are five Psalms that are classified as salvation history Psalms: 78, 105, 106, 135, and 136. They all contain a long series of verses and stanzas that record in chronological order many of the great deeds of God on behalf of the people. Psalms 78, 105, and 106 are clearly didactic. Psalm 135 is more like a hymn of praise, and Psalm 136 is presented in the form of a litany. Both of these Psalms were most likely used in the corporate worship services of the people.

4. Psalms of the Lord as King

These Psalms are also referred to as *enthronement Psalms* suggesting the enthronement of God as the King of Israel. There are many Psalms that refer to a king. The psalms of this type all focus on God as the King. These Psalms are a reminder of the time when Israel's only king was the Lord God. Yet, the Israelites kept pleading for a king to rule them like their neighbors, and Samuel was anointed as the first King of Israel. Kings rise and fall, but only God continues as the sovereign ruler over the people. Only God is worthy of the praise, devotion, and allegiance that the people offer to their king. Here is a very good example of this psalm type:

The Lord is King.
   He is clothed with majesty and strength.
The earth is set firmly in place
   and cannot be moved.
Your throne, O Lord, has been firm from
      the beginning,
   and you existed before time began.
The ocean depths raise their voice, O Lord;
   they raise their voice and roar.
The Lord rules supreme in heaven,
   greater than the roar of the ocean,
   more powerful than the waves of the sea.
Your laws are eternal, Lord,
   and your Temple is holy indeed,
   forever and ever.

                                        Psalm 93

5. Hymns of Zion
(Praise of Jerusalem, the Holy City)

As God the King is to be praised, so is the place of God's abode, Jerusalem—the holy city, the sacred hill, the place where the Temple was built. There are several Psalms that refer to Zion as the special place where God is present. Zion is one of the hills on which Jerusalem stands. Apparently a fortress was built on the hill to protect the city. When David became king he captured "their fortress of Zion, and it became known as 'David's City' " (II Samuel 5:7). The Ark of the Covenant was brought by David to Jerusalem to symbolize God's presence in the midst of the people. *Zion* is often used to refer to the whole of the city of Jerusalem and also may be used in the sense of the people of Jerusalem as

a community whose destiny is governed by God. Today the Zionist movement is a nationalistic movement of the Jewish people who continue to claim Jerusalem and Israel as a city and nation of God's own eternal choosing. Here is an example of a "Hymn of Zion":

The Lord is great and is to be highly praised
   in the city of our God, on his sacred hill.
Zion, the mountain of God, is high and beautiful;
   the city of the great king brings joy to all the world.
God has shown that there is safety with him
   inside the fortresses of the city.
The kings gathered together
   and came to attack Mount Zion.
But when they saw it, they were amazed;
   they were afraid and ran away. . . .

People of God, walk around Zion and count
      the towers;
   take notice of the walls and examine the fortresses,
so that you may tell the next generation:
   "This God is our God forever and ever;
he will lead us for all time to come."

                                 Psalm 48:1-5, 12-14

6. Royal Psalms (The King of Israel)

We have already encountered Psalms that refer to God as King of Israel. In these royal Psalms the focus is on the reigning king of Israel, not God. This psalm type is determined by the content, the focus on the king, not the structure. Among the royal Psalms are quite a variety of situations in which the king is involved. Psalm 18 describes the king expressing thanksgiving for victory over his enemies. Psalm 20 is a prayer on behalf of the king's safety as he goes to battle. Psalm 21 is another hymn of thanksgiving for the Lord's protection of the king in battle. Psalm 45 hails the king on the occasion of his marriage. Several Psalms (2, 72, and 110) refer to the king's ascension to the throne and may have been used in a liturgy celebrating the anniversary of his ascension. The last of the royal Psalms is 101, which is written in first-person narration as a series of vows or promises made by the king to the Lord.

7. Individual Psalms of Lament

There are more individual Psalms of lament (approximately forty) than there are any other type. These appear throughout the whole anthology of one hundred fifty Psalms. The essential clues to this type being classified as *individual* Psalms of lament are the key words: *I, me,* and *my*. The laments are all personal concerns of an individual, even if the individual is a representative of a whole community. Most of the psalms of this type have similar elements. There is an *address* to God and a *cry* for God's help. In order for a Psalm to be a lament, there must be an *expression of distress* but the exact cause or nature of the distress is more often than not unclear. Accompanying each lament are words of *supplication* with reasons why the Lord should intervene on behalf of the Psalmist. Many of the individual Psalms of lament conclude with a *vow to praise*.

In these Psalms of lament we experience the deepest emotions of the Psalmist where there are expressions of abandonment, defeat, despair, grief, agony, sorrow, and betrayal. Often the laments are prefaced by the cry, "How long, O Lord, how long . . . ?" An excellent example of a brief individual lament is Psalm 13.

How much longer will you forget me, Lord? Forever?
  How much longer will you hide yourself from me?
How long must I endure trouble?
  How long will sorrow fill my heart day and night?
  How long will my enemies triumph over me?

Look at me, O Lord my God, and answer me.
  Restore my strength; don't let me die.
Don't let my enemies say, "We have defeated him."
  Don't let them gloat over my downfall.

I rely on your constant love;
  I will be glad, because you will rescue me.
I will sing to you, O Lord,
  because you have been good to me.

Other examples of individual Psalms of lament include: 5-7, 17, 22, 35, 41-43, 51, 54-57, 69, 86, 102, and 140-143. (See the index for the complete list, and see chapter 16 for more information regarding this type.)

8. Community Psalms of Lament

This is the third most familiar type with approximately fifteen Psalms identified as community Psalms of lament. The personal refer-ences in this type are corporate using the key words: *we, us,* and *our*. The cause of the distress prompting the lament usually has something to do with the enemy, the wicked ones, a natural calamity, the sinfulness of the people, or God's own judgment. The common elements in many of the community laments are a description of the *distress,* and *appeal to God* for his assistance, an *expression of trust* in God, as the Psalmist on behalf of the people remembers God's past actions and a *vow or promise* to offer thanksgiving for God's deliverance. The lament moves from brokenness to wholeness, from complaint to praise, from despair to joy. Israel's history is formed and interpreted as a continual experience of reaching out to God, seeking his aid, and God's responding with redemption and deliverance.

Psalm 79 provides a good example of the elements of this type of psalm as the following four verses illustrate:

O God, the heathen have invaded your land.
They have desecrated your holy Temple
  and left Jerusalem in ruins.

Lord, will you be angry with us forever?
  Will your anger continue to burn like fire?

Do not punish us for the sins of our ancestors.
  Have mercy on us now; we have lost all hope.
Help us, O God, and save us;
  rescue us and forgive our sins. . . .

Then we, your people, the sheep of your flock,
  will thank you forever
  and praise you for all time to come.
                              Psalm 79:1, 5, 8-9, 13

Included in the community laments are Psalms 12, 44, 58, 60, 74, 80, 83, 85, 89, 90, 94, 123, 129, and 137.

9. Psalms of Trust

In a sense this category is artificial because all of these Psalms could be included in one or another of the various types we are exploring. However, as I read the Psalms I am impressed over and over again with the trust—the absolute dependence the Psalmist has in his creator, redeemer God. The content of these Psalms seems to transcend all of the intervening centuries. I can read or pray the Psalms of trust out of my own faith journey and feel them to be as relevant to me today as they must have been to the Psalmist over twenty-four centuries ago and as they have been for God's people of every generation since. These Psalms serve as an excellent resource for personal devotions and corporate worship. In many ways these Psalms serve as affirmations of our faith in God as protector, redeemer, Lord, and sustainer.

The Twenty-third Psalm is the most familiar of this type and has been memorized by more believers than any other Psalm. There are about a dozen other Psalms of trust, and they can be illustrated by another Psalm that is familiar to many, Psalm 121.

I look to the mountains;
    where will my help come from?
My help will come from the Lord,
    who made heaven and earth.

He will not let you fall;
    your protector is always awake.

The protector of Israel never dozes or sleeps.
The Lord will guard you;
    he is by your side to protect you.
The sun will not hurt you during the day,
    nor the moon during the night.
The Lord will protect you from all danger;
    he will keep you safe.
He will protect you as you come and go
    now and forever.

By the rivers of Babylon we sat down;
    there we wept when we remembered Zion.
On the willows near by
    we hung up our harps. . . .
How can we sing a song of the Lord
    in a foreign land?
May I never be able to play the harp again
    if I forget you, Jerusalem!

Psalm 137:1-2, 4-5

Other Psalms included in Psalms of trust are Psalms 11, 16, 23, 26, 31, 62, 63, 91, 131, and 139.

10. Torah Psalms (Praising the Law of God)

The Hebrew word *torah* means literally "teachings." Torah Psalms refer to the laws of God that find their origin in the commandments received by Moses and developed fully in the Pentateuch, commonly called the Books of Moses. These books were also referred to in the canon as the Law. There are only two psalms of this type: Psalm 19:7-14 and the longest of all, Psalm 119. As noted in the previous chapter, Psalm 119 is composed of twenty-two stanzas of eight lines each, with each stanza beginning with a different letter of the Hebrew alphabet. The twenty-two stanzas are redundant, as each one speaks of the importance of the Law in a similar way. The Law, its importance, the benefits of devotion to it, and the consequences of not obeying it are essential elements of each stanza. Some students of Psalms assign the two Torah Psalms to the same category as the Wisdom Psalms. The only thing gained by combining these two types of psalms is reducing the number of types. I believe Psalm 119 is substantial enough in terms of its content, as well as its length, to deserve a category of its own.

11. Wisdom Psalms

Wisdom Psalms are not an easily definable type. Many of the wisdom Psalms can be classified with other types. However, the ten or so wisdom Psalms are sufficiently compatible with each other as to deserve their own designation. Wisdom Psalms are often much like proverbs—with short, memorable sayings of common wisdom. When searching for wisdom Psalms, we notice the contrasting of the righteous with the wicked, the light with the darkness, the good with the evil. This contrasting is characteristic of wisdom passages. Some other elements of wisdom Psalms are: advice concerning personal behavior, the "blessed formula," the use of comparisons and admonitions, the address to a son, or mentioning the fear of the Lord. In most of the wisdom Psalms each pair of lines, or verse, usually stands alone and is not directly related to the verses before or after.

Psalm 127 serves as a good representative of wisdom Psalms.

If the Lord does not build the house,
　the work of the builders is useless;
if the Lord does not protect the city,
　it does no good for the sentries to stand guard.
It is useless to work so hard for a living,
　getting up early and going to bed late.
For the Lord provides for those he loves,
　while they are asleep.
Children are a gift from the Lord;
　they are a real blessing.
The sons a man has when he is young
　are like arrows in a soldier's hand.
Happy is the man who has many such arrows.
He will never be defeated
　when he meets his enemies in the place of
　　judgment.

Features of the wisdom Psalms can also be observed in Psalms 1, 34, 36, 37, 49, 73, 112, 127, and 128.

12. Liturgical Psalms

Many Psalms have been and continue to be used in the liturgies of God's people as they gather for worship. The Psalms have been sung as hymns, offered as prayers, recited in unison, responsively and antiphonally, and read as the scripture lesson. In reviewing the Psalms and reading commentaries about them, one discovers that some of the Psalms appear to have originated in some festival or other special worship experience of the Jewish people. Psalms 84 and 122 indicate that the worshipers are involved in a pilgrimage to Jerusalem and the Temple, "How I love your Temple, Lord Almighty! How I want to be there! I long to be in the Lord's Temple . . ." (84:1-2). There are two Psalms (15 and 24) that appear to be entrance liturgies that were used as the worshipers stood outside the gates of the Temple awaiting entrance.

Who has the right to go up the Lord's hill?
　Who may enter his holy Temple?
Those who are pure in act and in thought,
　who do not worship idols or make false
　　promises. . . .

Fling wide the gates, open the ancient doors,
    and the great king will come in.
Who is this great king?
    He is the Lord, strong and mighty . . .
Fling wide the gates, open the ancient doors,
    and the great king will come in.

                              Psalm 24:3-4, 7-9

We have already placed Psalm 136 among the salvation history Psalms. However, it also could be included with the liturgical Psalms because of its form. It is clearly a litany where the second line of each verse of the Psalm is a corporate response, "for his [the Lord's] steadfast love endures for ever" (RSV). No doubt Psalm 136 was used in its beginning as part of the worship experience of the Jewish people. Three other Psalms are representative of this type: 81, 115, and 118.

Practice Identifying Psalm Types

Having been introduced to the twelve types of psalms, the participants are now ready to do some analyzing on their own. Prepare a set of instructions on a transparency or sheet of newsprint so that the members of the study group can spend ten to fifteen minutes working with selected Psalms to see if they are able to classify them by type.

After participants have had enough time to work on the task, the leader/teacher should provide enough time for the small groups to share their findings and compare notes with others in the group. It is possible there will be differences of opinion in deciding which type a particular psalm represents. The important thing is not to force persons to agree with the teacher/leader, but rather we should be open to hearing what clues within the Psalm led persons to make their judgments. Based upon the evidence cited, the leader/teacher may agree with the choices. It is also important to share with the participants why another designation could be made for the same Psalm. All of us should be quite open to a variety of interpretations and expressions of opinion.

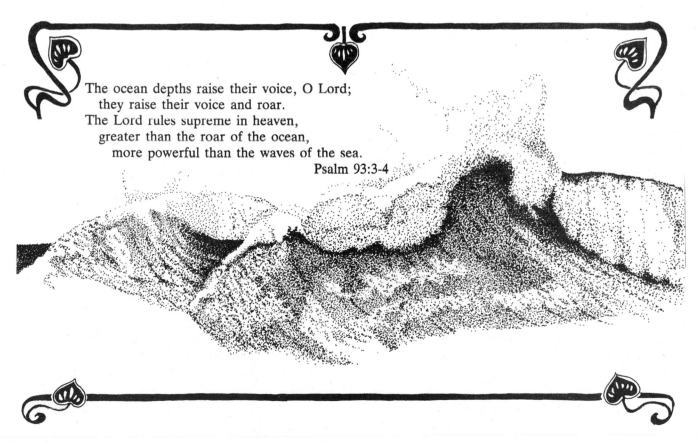

The ocean depths raise their voice, O Lord;
    they raise their voice and roar.
The Lord rules supreme in heaven,
    greater than the roar of the ocean,
    more powerful than the waves of the sea.
                    Psalm 93:3-4

WORKSHEET

Directions

1. Work with another person or two.

2. Select four to six of the following Psalms:

1	16	29	72	93	118
2	19:7-14	34	74	95	119
7	20	37	76	96	125
8	23	46	78	103	136
11	24	47	84	104	138
13	25	60	85	105	

3. Read the Psalms to try to identify which of the twelve types each one represents.

4. Be prepared to share your observations with others in the group.

13

Psalms Praising God the Creator

Setting the Stage

This teaching activity focuses on the four Psalms of creation: 8, 19:1-6, 104, and 148. It is important to read the brief description of this psalm type in chapter 12. The teacher/leader will find it helpful to read one or more commentaries to become familiar with how the biblical scholars interpret these four Psalms.

The activity presents a session plan that will require about ninety minutes, if all of the steps are to be completed without the participants feeling rushed. In addition to the four Psalms of creation, participants will spend some time with the first two chapters of Genesis in order to compare those narratives of creation with the four Psalms.

Since the focus is on God the creator and on the creation, it seems most appropriate to involve the participants in doing a little creating themselves. The size of the group, the time available, the previous experiences of the participants with creative activities, and the resources at hand all will influence the planning of the leader/teacher. This session plan suggests an outline of several possible creative activities. There are many other possibilities. The essential concern is that the participants become involved in some form of creative activity. Whether there are a number of options from which to choose or the whole group does the same activity is not as critical as involving everyone in some experience of creativity.

Opening

Begin the session by reading in unison Psalm 8 from the *Good News Bible*.

Have available a collection of photographs or teaching pictures that present a variety of expressions of the universe, world of nature, and people that God has created. There should be more photographs than participants so that everyone will have a variety to choose from.

Encourage each individual to select *one* photograph that depicts God as creator. After participants select photographs they return to their seats and spend a few moments in silence "reading" the photograph. As they continue to view the photograph, the teacher/leader guides them in a brief meditation, using questions like:

1. What beauty do you see in God's creation?
2. What power do you see in God's creation?
3. To what extent is God's creation quite fragile?
4. What is the importance of what you are viewing to the created order?
5. What responsibilities do you and others have for preserving, fulfilling, and using this aspect of God's creation?
6. What words of praise and thanksgiving would you use in a prayer responding to God for what God has created?

(Allow thirty seconds of silence after asking each question so that participants will have time to think, reflect, and meditate.)

Immediately following the time of meditation, invite participants to write brief prayers of praise and thanksgiving. The prayers can then be read and shared in the form of a litany using a corporate response such as, "O God, hear our prayer."

Compare Two Creation Narratives

Before looking at the Psalms of creation, we will review the two creation narratives in the first and second chapters of Genesis.

The large group will be divided into smaller groups of four-six persons each. With a class of fewer than six persons, the class can work as one small group. Half of each small group will work with Genesis 1:1-2:3, and the other half will work with Genesis 2:4-45. Working with their respective passages, each group will answer the following questions based solely on the evidence gained from their passage.

1. What element of time is stated?
2. What is the "location" or place of creation?
3. What is the order in which things are created?
4. When in the process was the man created?
5. When in the process was the woman created?
6. What is the relationship between the created order and God?
7. What is the relationship of humankind to the rest of creation?
8. What is the essential message of the passage?

Two or three persons in the small groups can compare notes to answer the questions based on their passage and then compare their answers with the small group working on the other passage. If there is sufficient time the leader/teacher can make a composite of the answers from both creation narratives on a transparency or newsprint sheet. The whole group should be well-equipped to reflect on the results of their investigation. They can be guided in their discussion with questions such as:

1. What impressions do you have as you compare the two sets of answers?
2. How would you characterize or summarize one narrative as compared to the other?
3. How would you account for the differences between the two narratives and their placement side-by-side in Genesis?
4. What would you identify to be a common affirmation of the two narratives?
5. In what ways are both narratives true?

Praise the Lord! . . .
Praise him, sun and moon,
　praise him, shining stars.
Praise him, highest heavens,
　and the waters above the sky.

Psalm 148:3-4

6. Why do you suppose the Hebrews worshiped the creator rather than the creation?

Work with Two Psalms

There are four Psalms that are identified as Psalms of creation: 8, 19:1-6, 104, and 148. We read in unison Psalm 8 as part of the opening. Have everyone look at Psalm 8 and 19:1-6 for just a few minutes to reflect on two questions: (1) What similarities or differences are there between these two Psalms and the Genesis narratives?, and (2) What is the essential message expressed by each of the Psalms?

Psalms 104 and 148 are much longer than Psalms 8 and 19 and contain much more with which to work. There are several alternative strategies from which the teacher/leader can choose in order to develop this step:

1. Divide the group into the same smaller groups as before, or divide into different smaller groups so that participants will have the pleasure of working with a new partner or two. Give each small group one of the two Psalms, 104 or 148. As they read the Psalm, use the same eight questions that guided the review of the Genesis creation narratives. Answer as many questions as are appropriate. Compare notes and share answers in the smaller groups or with the whole group.

2. Encourage participants to work individually with both Psalms using the same eight questions as a guide for reflecting on the Psalms. Compare notes and share answers in smaller groups or with the whole group.

3. The teacher/leader can work with the class as a whole, working with one Psalm at a time. The eight questions can be asked one at a time, which may encourage participants to speak up and share with everyone their insights or observations.

A key question to ask, no matter which of the three strategies is used, is, "Which of the two Genesis narratives is more closely linked to the Psalm passage?" Several of the six questions that were used earlier to guide discussion of the Genesis narratives can be used again to draw together insights about these two Psalms.

Creating with Words, Clay, or Images

A lot of time has been spent exploring verbally and conceptually the insights gained from Genesis and Psalms regarding God the creator and the creation. Now is the time for a little creativity. There are many materials and processes that can be suggested to involve persons creatively. I have outlined three possibilities. Those using this activity outline can adapt, sustitute, or add to these three creative activities. All three activities can be offered to one group, if the group is large enough. Each participant can then choose which of the three activities to experience. However, just one of the three can be offered to the group so that everyone is working on the same activity simultaneously.

1. Creating with Words

Participants can use a poetry form such as cinquain or haiku to create their own poems. Or they can write poems without a rigid form by following the style and form of the Psalmist in Psalms 104 or 148.

Cinquain

The word *cinquain* refers to the number five. There are five lines in the poem. A *cinquain* is usually done with these guidelines.

Line 1	Title (a noun)	—
Line 2	Describes the title	— —
Line 3	Action words about the title	— — —
Line 4	Describes a feeling about the title	— — — —
Line 5	Refers back to the title	—

Haiku

The haiku is a poetry form that has come to us from Japan. Traditionally, haiku are written about some aspect of the natural world and the seasons of the year. Haiku consist of three, unrhymed, unmetered lines with five syllables in the first line, seven in the second, five in the third, or seventeen syllables in all.

The haiku poem is not expected to say everything about a subject. We are not concerned about complete sentences but about complete ideas. Through its seventeen concentrated syllables, the haiku has the power to evoke associations, images, and feelings in the listener who becomes a co-creator, sharing in the experiences of the writer.

— — — — —

— — — — — —

— — — — —

2. Creating with Clay

Clay is a marvelous medium that persons can use to shape, mold, sculpt, smash, and scratch in order to create an object that expresses something of their feelings and thoughts about God and creation. It is important to obtain a good quality potter's clay and not use children's modelling clay. The potter's clay responds so well to the working of our fingers. Even clay under the fingernails feels good. Also, arrangements can be made to fire the potter's clay so that the finished object can be made solid and permanent.

3. Creating with Images

Psalm 148 lends itself beautifully to being expressed visually with Write-On Slides. (Write-On Slides are a Kodak Ektagraphic product available from teachers' supply stores and audio-visual dealers). There are fourteen verses in Psalm 148. Each person in the group can illustrate a line, a verse, or two verses with one or two Write-On slides. After all the verses are illustrated, the slides can be projected while someone in the group slowly reads Psalm 148.

Closing

The session can be closed by:
1. Sharing the products of the creativity.
2. Praying/reading in unison or antiphonally Psalms 104 or 148.
3. Singing a hymn that celebrates God as Creator. Some possible hymns include:
   "Praise Ye, Praise Ye the Lord"
   "All Creatures of Our God and King"
   "I Sing the Almighty Power of God"
   "O Lord, Our Lord, in All the Earth"
   "The Spacious Firmament on High"
   "All Things Bright and Beautiful"

14

Psalms of the Mighty Acts of God

Setting the Stage

The focus of this activity is the tradition—the story of God's many and marvelous acts of choosing, loving, judging, and redeeming God's own people. The mighty acts of God are recalled briefly in many Psalms. However, there are four Psalms that deal specifically with a portion of the tradition (Psalms 78, 105, 106, and 136).

Tradition is a body of belief or a story of events that is communicated from one generation to the next. Tradition results from the process of hearing, remembering, affirming, and retelling The Story of our origins as a religion, a nation, or even as a family. Traditions are shared in story; acted out; expressed visually in painting, sculpture, and other mediums; celebrated in dance, festival, and worship; as well as composed in prose, poetic, or musical form. We know ourselves and are known by others according to the stories we create, remember, and tell about who we are. We are shaped by traditions we identify with, and we reshape those same traditions as we pass them on to others. When we know and affirm The Story of our people and experience ourselves as being a part of that same story, then we are in a position to be a link in the process of passing the tradition from our parents' generation to our children's generation.

If there had not been a tradition or a story, there would not now be a people of the old covenant, Israel, or of the new covenant, the Christian church, the Body of Christ. Central to the life of the people of Israel in every generation was the remembering and retelling of God's great deeds on their behalf. Important events in the life of the people (flood, covenant making, exodus, wars of victory and defeat, exile, and return) were all identified as times when God was acting in, for, and through the affairs of people and the dynamics of nature. The stories of God at work among the people and the people's relationships with God and others were stories formed, told, remembered, and retold to such an extent that events in centuries past became a part of the people's own personal stories of faith. To Hebrews of a later time, the account of, "A wandering Aramean was my father; and he went down into Egypt . . . " (Deuteronomy 26:5-9 RSV) was not just telling about Joseph's father but in a very real sense it was the story of their fathers.

There are no prophets, no preachers, no teachers without a story to tell—a tradition to maintain. Tradition is the source of the dependable message of what God has done and will do. Tradition is not just a focus on the past, but rather gives a sense of continuity, that God's mighty acts of the past will be realized in the present and continue in the future.

We live and work in a day when many of God's people have lost touch with the tradition—The Story of their ancestors in the faith. Just to do some remedial work by informing persons about some of the facts of The Story is not enough. Nor is it enough to select and remember a few significant Bible verses, lifting them out of their context and force-fitting them into contemporary situations of faith and life. What we need is living with the whole story—participating in The Story so completely that it becomes our story. When it becomes our own story, there is then a power and presence of God at work that not only transforms the tradition but also our lives, which in turn transforms the world.

With this teaching activity, we may get in touch with a part of the tradition of God's people from Abraham to David as we look closely at four specific Psalms. The teacher/leader will be helped by reading about this psalm type, which may be identified as salvation history Psalms, sacred history Psalms, or just plain history Psalms. Having some additional background on the psalm type as well as reading a commentary or two about these four Psalms will enable the leader/teacher to be more resourceful for the participants during the session.

Opening

Teachers/leaders beginning this session may want to use the following words as an introduction to help the participants get started:

In this session we are going to work in depth with four Psalms identified as salvation history Psalms. These are Psalms that tell some of the story of God's saving acts in delivering the people from oppression, defeat, and sin.

Before we work with these Psalms, we are going to spend a few minutes reflecting a little on our own personal histories. Consider for a moment your life from birth to the present. Make a list, in chronological order, of some of the significant events or periods of time that contribute to your life story. Think of events or periods of time . . .

—that provide meaning for your pilgrimage of faith.
—that were life-changing and challenging.
—that represent struggle or trial that you overcame.
—that represent excitement or joy.

With just a few key words or phrases to represent each item, make a list as long as you can in five or six minutes.

After the lists are completed, invite persons to look at their lists, reviewing and identifying those times when they felt God was especially present and involved in their lives or perhaps times when God seemed absent or removed. Place an asterisk or check mark next to each of those items.

This list will be used toward the end of the session, so encourage participants to set them aside and save them for later.

Presenting the Psalm Type

The four salvation history Psalms have several characteristics in common. Even though written in the poetic form, they essentially present a narrative or story that has a beginning and an ending. The events of the narrative are presented in chronological order. The four salvation history Psalms have strong didactic overtones and appear to have been used to instruct the people about their heritage and to help them remember that heritage. The basic content of each of the Psalms is the great deeds or mighty acts of God. These great deeds reveal God's love for, judgment of, and deliverance of the people with whom God had established the covenant of faith. The events that comprise the narrative are essential to Israel's own self-understanding as the people of God, as well as essential to understanding who God is.

In Psalm 78:1-6 we gain some clues as to the purpose of this psalm type.

> Listen, my people, to my teaching,
>   and pay attention to what I say.
> I am going to use wise sayings
>   and explain mysteries from the past,
>   things we have heard and known,
>   things that our [parents] told us.
> We will not keep them from our children;
>   we will tell the next generation
>   about the Lord's power and his great deeds
>   and the wonderful things he has done. . . .
>
> He instructed our ancestors
>   to teach his laws to their children,
> so that the next generation might learn them
>   and in turn should tell their children.

That is why we continue to tell The Story, "so that the next generation might learn . . . and in turn tell their children." Even though Psalm 78 is the only one of the four with such a preface, we can presume that the same words could be used to introduce the other three Psalms.

Note: In some lists Psalm 135 is included as a salvation history Psalm. I have chosen not to include Psalm 135 in this activity because it does not present The Story of God's mighty acts quite as clearly as the other four.

Exploring the Four Psalms

The total group is to be divided into four smaller groups. If the group is larger than twenty members, it may be more workable to have more smaller groups rather than there being more than five persons to a group. (With twenty-four participants there could be eight groups of three persons each.)

Provide the following directions:

Directions

1. Work with a small group with one of the following Psalms:

   78   105   106   136

2. As you read your Psalm consider several questions:
   —What are the beginning and ending points (events or persons) of the story?
   —In what other books of the Bible is this period of history recorded?
   —What are some of the connecting links that hold the whole story together as one story?
   —What do you think is the essential meaning or significance of this history?
3. Prepare brief answers to share with the whole group.

Comparing Answers

After the small groups have had sufficient time (ten-fifteen minutes) to read the Psalm and answer the questions, arrange for a way to share the information. What works best for me is preparing a transparency (a sheet of newsprint would serve just as well) with the four Psalms noted across the top and the four questions listed in the left margin. (See the composite answer sheet at the end of this activity for an example.)

Work with one question at a time, receiving reports from all four groups before proceeding.

When all questions have been answered and recorded, ask a question or two to guide the participants in reflecting on the process, on the four Psalms, and on the composite set of answers. Some questions could be:

1. What are some of your observations or impressions of this process and the results of our study?
2. Why do you suppose these are called salvation history Psalms? What is another title or two that would be appropriate?
3. How does this holy history compare with the kind of history with which we are more familiar?
4. If you were to compose a more contemporary history of God's people, what would be some features of that history?

Psalm 136

Now that we have become familiar with four salvation history Psalms, we will spend a few minutes with Psalm 136. Notice that Psalm 136 is composed of twenty-six brief statements, each followed by the same response, "[God's] love is eternal" (TEV), "for [God's] steadfast love endures for ever" (RSV) or "[God's] steadfast love is eternal" (*The Book of Psalms,* Jewish Publication Society). Several lines or statements all relate to a specific theme that together form a stanza. In Psalm 136 there are five stanzas:
1. Opening (1-3)
2. God the Creator (4-9)
3. God the Deliverer from Egypt (10-15)

4. God the Protector in Battle (16-22)
5. God the Deliverer from Enemies (23-25)

Verse 26 is a concluding call to give thanks. With a brief reminder of the structure of Psalm 136 and a few clues as to what will follow, the leader/teacher can guide the group's participation in reading/praying Psalm 136 as a litany or an antiphonal reading. This reading will bring closure to the previous study and also provide a pattern for the participants to follow as they write brief statements and stanzas expressing their own salvation history.

Writing Brief Prayers

Now is the time to return to the lists that were prepared by the participants in the opening activity of this session. They are to look at the items that were noted as being most significant and use them as a basis for writing their own statements. The statements should be brief. Each statement is completed by the refrain, "God's steadfast love endures forever." And several statements can focus on one event, period of time, or theme in order to form a stanza.

Sharing Prayers

After about five to eight minutes for writing, the participants can be invited to share their statements and prayers. After each line is shared the whole group will respond, "God's steadfast love endures forever."

The following is a sample composite sheet with responses from one study group using the previous activity.

Psalms	78	105	106	136
Questions				
1. Beginning and ending?	Pre-Exodus Bondage	Abraham	in Egypt	Creation
	Choosing of David	in Canaan	in Babylonian exile	end of forty years wandering
2. What other books in the Bible?	Exodus	Genesis to	Exodus	Genesis to
	I Kings	Joshua	Joshua	Deuteronomy
3. Connecting links?	God's faithfulness, anger, judgment, and mercy ——— Israel's rebellions, sins, and unfaithfulness	God's faith-fulness in keeping the covenant, promise, and protection	God's judgment and mercy	God's involvement in all of history
4. Meaning and significance?	To tell the story so future generations will remember	God keeps his covenant and rewards the faithful	Praying for salvation from exile	The steadfast love of the Lord endures forever

15

Psalms of Trust

Setting the Stage

The Psalms of trust are not a pure type. Many commentators include these Psalms among the laments, the thanksgivings, liturgies, or others depending on the dominant theme present in the Psalm. However, there is an element of trust or confidence in God that is expressed in some Psalms to such an extent that it seems to me we should look at these Psalms as a separate type. The Psalms of trust are clearly affirmations of faith in God as the one who defends, protects, saves, and provides refuge. Though some might make a different list than the one I have made, I include the following among the Psalms of trust: 4, 11, 16, 23, 26, 27, 31, 62, 63, 91, 121, 125, 131, and 146.

There is the element of lament among five of the Psalms (4, 25, 31, 62, and 63). The element of praise and thanksgiving is found in seven of the Psalms (4, 16, 26, 27, 31, 63, and 146). Thus, it is possible to classify these Psalms as a different type. However, there is a significant, if not dominant, expression of trust and confidence in the Lord as the one who will protect and save the faithful people in these Psalms.

Serving as a focus in these Psalms of trust is the belief in God as creator and the experience of God as the One who delivers the people from bondage and establishes them in a good land where God dwells with them. Because of the people's belief in and experience of God, the Psalmist can express for himself, as well as for all the people, his absolute dependence upon and trust in God. Each of the Psalms of trust expresses confidence. Some examples include:

When I lie down, I go to sleep in peace;
  you alone, O Lord, keep me perfectly safe.

Psalm 4:8

I trust in the Lord for safety.

Psalm 11:1

You, Lord, are all I have, and you give me all I need;
  my future is in your hands.

Psalm 16:5

The Lord protects me from all danger;
  I will never be afraid.

Psalm 27:1b

I wait patiently for God to save me;
  I depend on him alone.

Psalm 62:1

The Lord will protect you from all danger;
  he will keep you safe.

Psalm 121:7

There are beautiful metaphors in some of these Psalms that express the nature of God's protection and the Psalmist's sense of trust. The most familiar of course is Psalm 23 with its image of the shepherd. In Psalm 63 and 91 we have the images of being safe "in the shadow of God's wings" or "covered by God's wings," which suggest that God takes care of the people like a hen protects her chicks. The house of the Lord, the holy Temple, providing protection is a suggestion in Psalms 11, 23, 26, and 27. God's love surrounding the people like the mountains surrounding Jerusalem is an image presented in Psalm 125. God offering security to the people like a mother offering security to the child in her arms is the image in Psalm 131. In Psalm 27 the images of shelter, tent, and rock all suggest security and protection.

In the Psalms of trust, God's actions are most often expressed with verbs such as *protects, saves, helps, loves, shelters, guides,* and *rewards.* In contrast and in response to God's actions, the people's actions are described by verbs such as: *trusts, loves, hopes, obeys,* and *praises.*

Reading the thirteen Psalms of trust that have been included in this category, we find two different stances or approaches taken by the Psalmist. On the one hand some of the Psalms of

The Lord is my shepherd;
   I have everything I need.
He lets me rest in fields of green grass
   and leads me to quiet pools of fresh water.
He gives me new strength.
He guides me in the right paths,
   as he has promised.

Psalm 23:1-3

trust are presented as prayers offered to God by the Psalmist or by the people. Psalms 4, 16, 23:4-6, 26, 27:7-14, 31, 63, and 131 are clearly prayers to God. On the other hand there are Psalms of trust that speak about God in the third person. It is as if the Psalmist is speaking to others about God rather than speaking directly to God. Psalms with this characteristic are 11, 23:1-3, 27:1-6, 62, 91, 121, 125, and 146. For the Psalmist, as well as for us today, it is important to communicate directly to God, expressing what we believe and feel about our relationship with the Lord Almighty *and* to communicate with others what we understand about our relationship to and belief in God. Such communication declares who God is, who we are, and what our relationship to God is.

In this activity participants will have the opportunity to explore the Psalms of trust as a type, as well as to spend time working with two Psalms in depth. It will be helpful for the participants to have access to Bible dictionaries and concordances. Several translations of the Bible also will provide additional insights.

Opening

If sufficient time is available, an excellent way to open this session is to use Praying Activity Two: Psalms for Personal Meditation. Six Psalms of trust are included in that praying activity. The leader also may select Psalms for personal meditation that are exclusively from the thirteen Psalms of trust.

Another way to open the session is to focus on Psalm 23. The group can be guided to either recite Psalm 23 from memory or read it in unison. Following the reading can be a singing of a hymn based upon this Psalm. Several appropriate hymns are: "The Lord's My Shepherd, I'll Not Want," "The King of Love My Shepherd Is," and "He Leadeth Me: O Blessed Thought."

The leader can ask questions in order for the participants to reflect on Psalm 23 in preparation for working with other Psalms of trust.

1. In what ways does the image of a shepherd help or hinder your thinking about and relating to God today?
2. What attributes of God do you see expressed in Psalm 23?

3. In what sense do you see Psalm 23 to be an affirmation of faith? What do we learn about making such an affirmation?
4. Why do you think Psalm 23 is included in the Psalms of trust category?

Exploring the Psalms of Trust

As was suggested in the "Setting the Stage" section, there are two different approaches taken by the Psalmist in the Psalms of trust: (1) prayers addressed to God and (2) words spoken about God. Each of these approaches is represented by the two different lists of Psalms in the following directions. It is important for all of the Psalms to be studied, but it does not make much difference how many groups work with the same Psalm.

Directions

1. Work in small groups of two or three.

2. As a group, select *one* Psalm from *each* of the two lists

A Psalm	B Psalm
4	11
16	27
23	62
26	91
31	121
63	125
131	146

3. Read the two Psalms that were selected and then reflect on the following questions:

   a. What difference do you notice between the two Psalms in terms of whom the Psalmist is addressing?

   b. What elements of other psalm types do you find in this Psalm? (Elements such as lament, petition, praise, and thanksgiving).

   c. What acts (actions) of God are expressed?

   d. What responses of the believer are expressed?

e. Which specific lines or verses of the Psalms would lead you to identify the two as Psalms of trust?

4. Prepare to share your findings with another small group or with the whole group.

After groups have had the opportunity to compare notes with each other, it is important for the leader to make some summary statements that would (1) state that this psalm type is not a pure type, (2) reinforce the fact that elements of other psalm types are present, (3) declare again the two approaches of the Psalmist in this type, and (4) suggest that there are several key words or phrases that are indicative of the Psalms of trust.

Word Study

The same groups continue to work together in this step.

The Psalms of trust are to some degree also affirmations of faith—affirmations of who God is and who the human being is in relation to God. There are several key words that appear a number of times in several of the Psalms of trust. The understanding of these key words can contribute much to our theology, our own affirmation of faith, and our way of interpreting these Psalms as well as other portions of scripture. The following directions for small groups working together will assist in the study of these key words.

Directions

1. Read again the two Psalms your group selected earlier. As you read, look to see if one or more of the following words (or synonyms for these words) appears:

protect	salvation
righteous	steadfast love
trust	safe
refuge	peace
life	hope
guides	death

2. Underline or otherwise note where these words or their synonyms occur in the two Psalms.

3. Using a Bible dictionary, concordance, commentary, word book, additional translations, or other resources, work with two or more of the words that appear most frequently or seem most significant. Develop a working definition of each word. It may work best if each individual works with a different word.

4. Reflect on several questions, and prepare to share your thoughts with others.
   a. How critical is the key word to understanding the message of the Psalm?
   b. With an understanding about God and the believer based upon the key word's concept, what is something important that is missing?
   c. In what setting or for whom would the particular Psalm and the developed interpretation be most helpful?

Take time for sharing by all the groups. It is expecially important to share the working definitions developed for the key words. The group can work with one Psalm at a time so that the important concepts of each Psalm are presented to the whole group.

Writing an Affirmation of Faith

Now that the Psalms of trust have been explored and key concepts have been understood, the participants should be ready to do some writing to express their own faith and trust in God. There are several suggestions to guide the writing. One suggestion can be chosen and used by all the participants. Or, all three ways can be offered as options so that the participants can select the one they prefer.

1. Use one of the Psalms that was explored as a basis for paraphrasing your own prayer to God or affirmation about God.
2. Use the Psalm format of short lines to write a poem or song that expresses trust in God.
3. Use the list of key words given earlier and include as many of the words as possible in a paragraph or two that will be either a prayer to God or a statement about God.

Time should be provided for individuals to share what they have written if they want to.

16

Psalms Lamenting Personal Distress

Setting the Stage

If you have been using the activities in the sequence presented, then I hope you have noticed that there is a rationale for the sequence. After the two general, introductory activities, we focused on the creation Psalms. Not only is creation a logical beginning, but belief in God as creator was one of the central tenets of the Hebrew faith. Another tenet, and perhaps *the* central tenet of the Hebrew faith was believing God to be the One who acted within history for the selection, leading, judging, and redeeming of the chosen people of God. Believing God to be Creator of all and Lord of history, the people not surprisingly put their trust and confidence in God. What comes next? If we believe God to be Creator, Lord, Redeemer, and Protector, then it follows that when all is not well and feelings of defeat and despair are dominant in our present experience, we should complain (or lament) to God expressing those feelings of abandonment.

The laments of the Psalmist communicate the deepest despair that can be expressed in words. The individual laments represent the largest number of Psalms of any one type, with approximately forty being so classified. Why so many Psalms of this one type? There is no clear-cut answer to that question. The geographical setting, the sociopolitical circumstances, the theological heritage, and the cultural climate all contributed to there being much for an individual to complain to God about. Since no one lived or died and no one succeeded or failed without God's intervention, then God is the One to whom all despairs, griefs, and concerns are expressed. With such factors very much present in the life and times of the Psalmist, it is not surprising that there are so many Psalms lamenting the distress of individuals.

Prayers of lament are the least common of the prayers expressed by the contemporary believer.

Today, we are more likely to curse God when things go awry. Cursing God is a way of dismissing God, renouncing our belief in God, or removing ourselves from God's authority. A curse arises out of disbelief rather than belief. This is quite unlike the laments that arise out of a belief in God as the One who is involved in all that happens. The bad things we experience may be attributed to enemies, to God, to others, or to self, but the person of faith affirms that God is the One who is able to protect, save, redeem, and restore wholeness.

This activity will attempt to help persons understand the nature of individual Psalms of lament in order to feel more comfortable with including the vocabulary of laments to God in their own prayers. This and the next activity on community Psalms of lament follow a similar format of (1) reviewing the characteristics of elements of the laments, (2) testing the elements against a sample Psalm, (3) working with selected Psalms to identify the elements of lament present in those Psalms, and (4) writing personal prayers of lament.

Opening

Some or all of what is included in the previous section, "Setting the Stage," can be shared with the participants as a way of opening this activity.

Another possibility is to ask participants what they think of when they first hear the word *lament*. Discussing common definitions as well as looking at some dictionary definitions may be a helpful way to get into the topic.

A third, inductive way to introduce the topic is to ask persons to think of events, persons, groups, or anything else that really bothers them a great deal. If there was a "complaint department" for the world, what serious complaint would be delivered? After participants have shared their complaints, the leader/teacher can make a smooth transition by suggesting that we are not the only ones with complaints. The Psalmist in ancient times had a lot of complaints also. These complaints are called laments and there are many Psalms that are known as individual Psalms of lament.

Presenting Elements of the Psalm Type

When one looks at the individual Psalms of lament as a whole, there are at least five elements that appear to be characteristic of this type. Not all elements are present in every Psalm, though. Nor do the elements appear in the same sequence in which they are presented here. However, the five elements are as follows:

1. *Invocation*
   The Psalmist addresses God—calls upon God to hear his prayer. Sometimes the invocation is as brief as "O Lord" and in other Psalms there is more to it, such as "O Lord, my God, I call for help by day; I cry out in the night before thee" (Psalm 88:1 RSV).
2. *Lament*
   Of course, the key words that distinguish these as individual laments are the first-person singular pronouns: *I, me, my,* and *mine.* The lament is a complaint or grievance addressed to God but occasioned by something that another person, the self, or God has done to cause the person distress. The specific circumstance causing the lament is seldom clear; however, the nature of the lament is often quite clear whether it be because of sin, abandonment by friends or by God, the actions of enemies, or personal sickness or grief.
3. *Expression of Confidence or Trust*
   As we suggested earlier, the Psalmist is able to express his deepest despair because he is confident of God's dependable presence and action on his behalf. In many of the laments of personal distress, the Psalmist expresses his confidence and trust with phrases that begin with, "the Lord is," "because of," "but I have trusted in," "I put my hope in," and "I have complete confidence, O God."
4. *Petition or Supplication*
   Accompanying each lament is a corresponding petition that asks God to do something. Knowing of God's past actions and having trust in God's presence, the Psalmist is quite confident in God's power and authority to act in response to his distress. The supplication is usually a very direct statement that begins with words such as: *hear, turn, restore, protect, come.* Often the petitions are punctuated with an exclamation point in the *Good News Bible,* the Bible in Today's English Version.
5. *Expression of Praise or Vow to Praise*
   Often in the last verse or two, there is a statement that expresses or promises praise by the Psalmist in response to who God is and what God has done. This element is missing from more of the individual Psalms of lament than are any of the other elements.

Testing the Five Elements with a Sample Psalm

Psalm 13 is an excellent example of an individual Psalm of lament. The teacher/leader can "walk through" the Psalm with the participants pointing out each of the five elements as they appear (see page 87).

Analyzing Psalms of Personal Lament

With the information provided in the previous step, the participants are now ready to look at some Psalms of personal lament to try to find as many of the five elements as possible. The directions to guide the participants are as follows:

Directions

1. Work in small groups of two or three.
2. Each group will work with *one* of the following Psalms of Lament.

Psalm	Psalm	Psalm
5	38	71
17	39	88
22	42	140
35	57	143

3. Read the Psalm and look for the five elements described earlier.
4. Each individual match up with four or five other persons who have worked with different Psalms to compare notes and share findings.

How much longer will you forget me, Lord?
  Forever?
How much longer will you hide
  yourself from me?
How long must I endure trouble?
How long will sorrow fill my
  heart day and night?
How long will my enemies
  triumph over me?

Look at me, O Lord my God,
  and answer me.
Restore my strength;
  don't let me die.
Don't let my enemies say,
  "We have defeated him."
Don't let them gloat over
  my downfall.

I rely on your constant love;
  I will be glad, because you will
    rescue me.
I will sing to you, O Lord,
  because you have been good to me.

1. "Lord" is the closest we have to an *invocation* in this Psalm.

2. The five statements that begin "how much" or "how long" are the *lament*.

3. We now have four lines of *petition*.

4. These two lines are the *expression* of *trust*.

5. The last line is a vow to *praise*.

My God, my God, why have you abandoned me?
I have cried desperately for help,
  but still it does not come. . . .
My cnemics surround me like bulls;
  they are all around me,
  like fierce bulls from the land of Bashan.
They open their mouths like lions,
  roaring and tearing at me.

                    Psalm 22:1, 12-13

After the small groups have done their work and have shared their findings with others, the teacher/leader should provide some time to respond to any questions participants might have or to hear their observations and insights.

If there is time, the participants can look at the same Psalm or a different one to reflect on several other questions:

1. What clues are there, if any, of the circumstances for the lament?

2. To what extent does the supplication match or relate to the lament?

3. With what elements or words of the Psalm do you identify most closely?

Writing a Personal Prayer of Lament

Before writing, the participants can be encouraged to think about an event; a set of circumstances in the church, community, or world; a person; or an experience that causes them to be distressed. They need to focus on something specific before they start writing.

With a specific concern in mind and using the five elements as an outline, each individual can write a personal prayer of lament. Provide about five to eight minutes for the writing.

To close the session, those who desire to can share their prayers of lament. After each prayer is shared, the group can respond with the words, "O Lord, by your grace, hear and answer this prayer." Amen.

17

Psalms Lamenting Community Distress

Setting the Stage

In response to defeat in battle, the destruction of Jerusalem and the Temple, or the threat of hostilities by the enemies, the Psalmist writes community Psalms of lament. The words of these Psalms are written by an individual. However, they are not written by the individual for himself but rather as an individual who is representative of the nation—who addresses God on behalf of all the people. Among Psalms there are about a third as many community laments (thirteen) as there are individual laments (about forty).

God was perceived by the Hebrew people as the One who is actively engaged in all their affairs as the people of the covenant. God was seen as the King who rules, who leads forth in battle against the enemy, and who establishes peace in the land. And, God was believed to have authority over all creation and all other nations. With such perceptions it is natural that God would be the One to whom the laments of the people would be addressed as they suffer defeat and experience much distress.

As with the individual laments, it is because of the Psalmist's absolute dependence upon and commitment to God that he is able to express his deepest feelings of distress to God without hesitation. There is no need to hide anything from God since God is already involved in the national, as well as the personal affairs of the people. Whether it is because of our sophistication or our arrogance, I am not sure which, but it is a fact that we seldom in the context of corporate worship express our laments to God. It is quite possible that our worship is less complete and honest when we withhold the anger, the disappointment, and the abandonment we feel that could very well be expressed as laments. I do not remember ever hearing or speaking a prayer of lament in the context of corporate worship. Yet, given the reality of wars and rumors of wars, of injustice at home and abroad, of the misuse of the environment and the economy, and of natural disasters all over the earth, it would be quite appropriate to express our laments to God.

Also, like the individual laments, the element of lament does not stand alone as the dominant factor in the community laments. The Psalmist expresses lament in the context of remembering God's past actions of deliverance, as well as affirming that God is the One with the authority and power to intercede on behalf of the faithful ones to bring them relief, renewal, or redemption. The Psalmist, speaking in the interest of the community, expresses a profound trust in God and thus is able to cry the lament without embarrassment or guilt.

This activity will follow a similar process as the one that focused on individual laments. It is possible to present this activity prior to the one on individual laments. It is also possible to combine the two activities or to do one of them in depth and the other more superficially. The time available, the needs and interests of the group, as well as the desires of the teacher/leader will all influence the direction to go with these two activities on laments.

Opening

If this activity follows the previous one, there is no need to spend much time introducing the concept of lament. With just a few words about the previous session, the group can start exploring community laments.

Another brief way to get into the subject is to ask participants to identify concerns in the church, community, nation, or world that really distress them. If there are any activists in the group who have supported a particular cause, they will not have any difficulty providing subjects for laments. It will be best if there are a variety of concerns expressed, so that at the end of the session, participants will have several options as they write their own community laments.

Presenting Elements of the Psalm Type

The elements of the community Psalms of lament have much in common with the individual Psalms of lament. Several of the elements are quite similar. Two of the elements are unique to the community laments: (1) remembering God's past acts and (2) questioning God. All of the elements are not present in every Psalm nor do they always appear in the same sequence as they are presented in this section. In most of the Psalms, there will be one element that is more prominent than the others; often that is the lament itself, but not always.

1. *Address to God*
   Except for Psalm 80 the community laments do not have a formal invocation, calling upon God to be present. In all of the other Psalms the address to God is simply, "O God," in the first line. Usually the "O God" is expressed in the context of a lament, a petition, or a remembrance of God's mighty deeds.

2. *Lament*
   Naturally, the distinguishing feature of the community laments is the use of the first-person plural pronouns such as: *we, us, our,* or *your* people. The Psalmist laments what is happening to the people, the nation—as a result of what the enemies are doing, what God is doing, or what the people themselves are doing. We can often presume what the circumstances are that give rise to the lament, even though the events are not clearly specified. We could expect that every psalm of this type would include explicit words of lament. However, such is not the case with Psalms 12 and 85 where the lament is more implied than it is stated directly. Reading between the lines of the petitions to God, we can detect the lament.

3. *Remembering God's Past Actions*
   In the individual laments there are expressions of trust and confidence in God. These expressions are, as we would expect, personal in nature. The community laments include something similar, though with more of a corporate or national perspective. In this type there is often a portion of the Psalm that recalls the mighty acts of God, which were accomplished for the people in the past. What we read is a brief salvation history. This element is never dominant in any of the

community laments, but it is present in at least half of them.

4. *Questioning of God*
Although this element is not identified as such by biblical scholars and commentators, it appears often enough to receive attention. The questions are stated in a variety of ways:

Have you really rejected us?
Aren't you going to march out with our armies? (60:10)

Lord, will you be angry with us forever?
Will your anger continue to burn like fire? (79:5)

Why did you break down the fences around it? (80:12*a*)

Who has felt the full power of your anger?
Who knows what fear your fury can bring? (90:11)

5. *Words of Affirmation*
In addition to remembering God's mighty acts of the past, there are words of affirmation that express for the Psalmist and the people their belief in God as One who creates, protects, leads, and forgives. Several of the Psalms include this element as we can see by the following examples.

You are my king and my God;
you give victory to your people.   (44:4)

With God on our side we will win;
he will defeat our enemies.   (60:12)

Surely [God] is ready to save those
who honor him.   (85:9*a*)

O Lord, you have always been our home.   (90:1)

6. *Petition*
Every community lament includes a petition that asks God to respond to the distress of the people. God's authority and power are never questioned, so the Psalmist assumes that God will be able to accomplish what is requested. The petitions all begin with words that suggest very specific actions, such as: help us, wake up, save us, remember, bring us back, turn to us, etc.

7. *Expressions of Praise*
There are only three of the community lament Psalms that include an expression of praise at the end.

Testing the Elements with a Sample Psalm

Since all of the community Psalms of lament are quite lengthy, there is not enough space in this segment to reproduce a sample Psalm. However, the leader/teacher can guide the group in looking for the seven elements in Psalm 60. The only hint of an address to God is the mention of God's name in verse 1. There are lines of lament in verse 1, 2, 3, and 4. The petitions to match each lament can be found in verses 1, 2, 5, and 11. Verses 6-8 present a review of some of the past mighty acts of God. The Psalmist questions God in verses 9 and 10. Psalm 60 concludes with an expression of trust in verse 12.

Analyzing Psalms of Community Lament

With the psalm type having been described and outlined, the participants are prepared to work independently with several representative Psalms, analyzing them for structure and content.

Directions

1. Work in small groups of two or three.
2. Each group will work with *one* of the following community laments:

Psalm	Psalm
44	80
58	83
74	85
79	90

3. Read the Psalm looking for the seven elements described earlier.
4. Each individual meets with another three or four persons who worked with different Psalms to compare notes and share findings.

When there has been opportunity for sharing findings and discussing questions that arise, the

How much longer, Lord God Almighty,
  will you be angry with your people's prayers?
You have given us sorrow to eat,
  a large cup of tears to drink.
You let the surrounding nations fight over our land;
  our enemies insult us.

Bring us back, Almighty God!
  Show us your mercy, and we will be saved!

Psalm 80:4-7

teacher/leader can conclude this part of the session by helping the participants reflect as a group on several questions:

1. What are some major emphases that appear to be different or similar when you compare the community laments with the individual laments?

2. As you read the community laments, what events or situations seem to have caused the lament?

3. To what extent would any of the laments be appropriately prayed in relation to the contemporary national or world scene?

Writing a Community Prayer of Lament

Now is the time to return to some contemporary concerns that were mentioned at the beginning of the session. Individuals should select one concern to be the focus of the community laments that they will write. Using all or some of the seven elements as an outline and writing brief statements that follow the format of the Psalms, the participants should be able to write their own community laments. After ten to fifteen minutes for writing, those who desire to should be encouraged to share their laments with the whole group.

18

Psalms of Praise and Thanksgiving

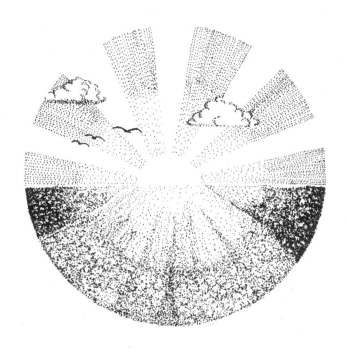

O Lord, our Lord,
your greatness is seen in all the world!

Psalm 8:1*a*

Setting the Stage

There are approximately twenty-five Psalms that have been included in the category of praise and thanksgiving, which makes this the second most common type after the individual Psalms of lament. These twenty-five are not the only Psalms to include the element of praise and thanksgiving. In one sense the ones we identified as creation Psalms and salvation history Psalms are also Psalms that praise God as creator and redeemer. The Psalms of lament often include an element of praise or thanksgiving in *anticipation* of what the Psalmist expects God to accomplish in response to the supplication. In the Psalms that we are specifically identifying as praise and thanksgiving, the praise and thanks to

God is usually in *response* to what God has already accomplished on behalf of the community (nation) or the individual.

Many of these Psalms of praise and thanksgiving may be more accurately referred to as songs or hymns than as prayers. It is often the case, is it not, that the hymns we sing are prayers expressed in a melody and tune, accompanied by piano, organ, or other musical instruments and sung in unison.

In most of the psalms of this type the phrase, "Praise the Lord," or a similar statement, appears in the opening verse. The words *thanks* and *thanksgiving* appear less often. However, it is very difficult to make a clear distinction between praise and thanksgiving, and that is the reason for including them together in this activity. It is because we are thankful that we offer our praise to God, and in our praise we show our thankfulness. In a number of Psalms the words *praise* and *thanks* appear together: 30:12; 33:1, 2; 95:1, 2; 100:4; 107:1, 2; 111:1; 116:17, 19; 138:1; and 145:1, 2.

There are two major sub-types of Psalms of praise and thanksgiving: (1) individual expressions and (2) community or corporate expressions of thanksgiving. In Psalm 66 we find a combination of the community and individual expressions. The praise and thankgiving offered to God are usually in response to: God's work as creator and sustainer; God's mighty acts as the One who chooses, guides, protects, loves, forgives, and redeems; and God's continuing presence in the affairs of the people.

As a response to all of these gracious acts of God, the Psalmist for himself as well as for the people offers much praise and thanksgiving.

The session opens with a time for praying and concludes with the writing of prayers of praise and thanksgiving. In the body of the teaching plan, there is time for exploring the structure of this psalm type.

Opening

To open the session the leader/teacher can provide a list of all the Psalms of praise and thanksgiving. (See index for the complete listing.) Direct the participants to skim as many of those Psalms as they can in a period of five to seven minutes. While skimming, they are to look for two or three verses that express their own prayers of praise and thanksgiving. Verses can be selected from more than one Psalm. It is important for persons to mark their verses in order to share them in a litany of praise and thanksgiving.

After giving time for skimming, the teacher/leader invites members of the group to read the verses of the Psalms they selected as their own prayers.

An excellent example and perhaps the text for this activity:

I will praise you, Lord, with all my heart;
  I will tell of all the wonderful things you have done.
I will sing with joy because of you.
  I will sing praises to you, Almighty God.
                                          Psalm 9:1-2

In response to each prayer that is shared, the group will say, "O God, how great you are!" or "O God, how worthy you are of our praise."

By skimming the Psalms of praise and thanksgiving, the participants receive an introduction to the psalm type and are now ready to explore it more thoroughly.

Presenting the Elements of the Psalm Type

In most of the Psalms of praise and thanksgiving, there are usually three major parts: (1) introduction, (2) the body of the Psalm, which often includes three other elements, and (3) the concluding ascription of praise. As with other psalm types, each Psalm does not necessarily include all of the elements, and the elements are not always presented in the same sequence.

1. *The Introduction*
   Words such as *ascribe* (29:1), *extol* (30:1), *make a joyful noise,* (66:1) and *bless* (103:1) in the Revised Standard Version are all translated as *praise* in the *Good News Bible.* The introduction is in the form of an address to God, declaring the Psalmist's intention to give praise and thanks. Psalm 30 provides a good example of this in the first verse, "I praise you, Lord, because you have saved me. . . ." In most of these Psalms there is a stated or implied "because," which gives the reason why we should praise God.

2. *The Body of the Psalm*
   The main body of the Psalm includes one or more of three elements:
   a) A *past distress* of the individual or the community is described. The difference between this element and a lament is that in the lament, the Psalmist is in the midst of trouble, has not experienced a resolution, and asks God to do something. In the Psalms of praise and thanksgiving, the distress has been resolved—God has already acted. In response to God's action the Psalmist offers praise and thanksgiving. In Psalm 30 we read, "my enemies from gloating . . . I was on my way to the depths below" (1, 3).
   b) A second element is the *plea* expressed by the Psalmist as he seeks God's help. This is not so much a petition as it is the Psalmist

remembering that he had called upon God to do something in the past. Words that express this element in Psalm 30 are: "I cried . . . I called . . . I begged . . . Hear me, Lord."

c) And, a third element is the *recollection of God's gracious deeds* that delivered the Psalmist or the people from their distress. This element is not unlike the longer salvation history Psalms or the element in the Psalms of lament that remembers God's past actions. Here, also, the Psalmist reminds himself and the people of the mighty acts of God, and it is in response to those acts that he must offer praise and thanksgiving. Again, in Psalm 30 we have examples of this element: "you healed me . . . you restored my life . . . you protected me . . . you have changed my sadness into a joyful dance." How God must be pleased by such an exuberant, devoted spirit.

3. *Ascription of Praise*

More than half of the psalms of this type have a concluding line, verse, or stanza declaring the Psalmist's praise and thanks in acknowledgement for all that God has done to preserve the people. Often the expression is simply, "Praise the Lord!" Psalm 30 gives an example of this element also: "So I will not be silent; I will sing praise to you. Lord, you are my God; I will give you thanks forever" (12).

When we read Psalm 30 from the first to the last verse, we can see that all the elements described above are present, but they do not appear in a neat one-two-three sequence. This is the case with all the Psalms of praise and thanksgiving—we will not find all of the elements in most of them. What we will always find, however, is a call, a promise, or an outburst of praise and/or thanksgiving.

Working with Psalm 107

Psalm 107 is one of the longer Psalms of praise and thanksgiving and, therefore, difficult to work with when it is included with some of the others. However, Psalm 107 has a striking structure; its content is quite provocative, and it contains good examples of all the elements except for the ascription of praise. To explore this Psalm quickly and in order to involve everyone, divide the verses among four small groups. Another strategy is for teachers/leaders to present the results of the work in a brief presentation as the participants read along in their own Bibles.

Directions

1. Work with one of four groups.

2. Everyone read Psalm 107:1-3 and 33-43.

3. Each group will then read and work with separate portions of Psalm 107.

   Group 1   Verses 4-9
   Group 2   Verses 10-16
   Group 3   Verses 17-22
   Group 4   Verses 23-32

4. As you read your portion of the Psalm, try to determine:

   a. Who is the subject?
   b. What is the distress?
   c. What is the plea to God?
   d. What is God's response?
   e. What is the people's response?

5. Finally, what relationship do you see between the portion you read and verses 1-3 and 33-43?

Except for step 5, it should not take much time to do the assignment. There is no clear-cut answer to the question in step 5. Some scholars suggest that verses 33-43 form a hymn praising the providence of God and may have been added to the rest of the Psalm later.

Some observations that should be made as a result of the study include:

1. There are four different groups of people who are the subjects of the four main stanzas: (a) travelers, (b) released prisoners, (c) those who were healed, and (d) seafarers.

2. The pattern of each stanza is the same with expression of distress, a plea to God, a subsequent deliverance, and finally an expression of thankfulness.

3. In each stanza there is a double refrain: "Then in their trouble they called to the Lord,

and he saved them from their distress.
"They must thank the Lord for his constant love,
for the wonderful things he did for them.

Analyzing Psalms of Praise and Thanksgiving

We have looked at two of the Psalms of praise and thanksgiving. It is not feasible to work with the more than twenty other Psalms, so the following part of the session involves individuals with one of ten selected Psalms. The intention of this step is to enable the participants to work inductively analyzing a Psalm and to share the results of their work with others. If the group is rather small the teacher/leader may want to limit the number of Psalms.

Directions

1. Individually select one of the following Psalms of Praise and Thanksgiving:

33	100	138
66	111	145
92	116	147
		149

2. Read the Psalm carefully and try to determine:
   a. which elements appear in the Psalm.
   b. the extent to which praise or thanks are present in the Psalm.
   c. the relevance of the Psalm to the present personal or corporate experiences of faith and life.

After working ten minutes with the Psalms, each individual can join with three or four others who analyzed different Psalms in order to share their findings with one another.

Write a Prayer of Praise and Thanksgiving

Using the form (introduction, expressions of distress, appeal to God for help, recalling God's past deliverance from distress, and concluding with praise) as a guide, the participants are invited to spend five to eight minutes writing their own prayers of thanksgiving. To get started, ask the participants to reflect on their own past experiences and to recall a time of personal or corporate distress when God's gracious intervention brought relief or resolution. The basic goal is to write four to seven sentences that incorporate elements of the psalm type they are working with. Participants should be reminded that the form of the prayer is not intended to limit their creative expression but rather to suggest what may be emphasized.

Provide time for those who want to share their prayers toward the end of this session.

Sing a Hymn of Praise or Thanksgiving

There are many hymns of praise and thanksgiving that find their origin in Psalms. The leader or a member of the group can assist in leading the singing of a hymn. If hymnals are not available, then the words to one or more stanzas of one or more hymns can be duplicated or printed on a song chart. The singing of a hymn of praise and thanksgiving would be a very effective way to conclude this session. Some examples of appropriate hymns are:

"O Lord, by Thee Delivered" (Ps. 30)
"Come, Ye That Fear the Lord" (Ps. 66)
"It Is Good to Sing Thy Praises" (Ps. 92)
"O Come and Sing unto the Lord" (Ps. 95)
"All People That on Earth Do Dwell" (Ps. 100)
"Praise the Lord, for He Is Good" (Ps. 107)
"Praise God, Ye Servants of the Lord" (Ps. 113)
"O Lord, Thou Art My God and King" (Ps. 145)
"Praise Ye, Praise Ye the Lord" (Ps. 148)

19

Studying a Psalm in Depth

Setting the Stage

All of the previous teaching activities have either provided background for Psalms in general or have dealt with a particular psalm type. In this activity we are going to work with one Psalm to suggest a way of approaching any particular Psalm. This activity can serve as a model for a whole series of sessions on individual Psalms. The approach to studying a Psalm in depth can be guided by eight questions we should ask of the Psalm as well as ourselves. These eight questions are applicable to any Psalm.

1. *What is the psalm type?*
   Identifying the Psalm by type provides a number of clues for interpreting it.
2. *What are the Psalm's distinguishing features?*
   The distinguishing features are the Psalm's structure, setting, author, style, etc.
3. *Where do the cross-references lead?*
   When we track down other places where parts of the Psalm are quoted, we gain some insight as to its use elsewhere in the Bible.
4. *What are the key words and concepts?*
   By focusing on the key words and concepts, we can begin to make some judgments about the message of the Psalm.
5. *How is the Psalm presented in other translations?*
   By reading two or more translations of the Psalm, we may increase our understanding of key words as well as our understanding of the whole Psalm.
6. *How is the Psalm interpreted by others?*
   It is important to consult commentaries and monographs that present the interpretations of others.

7. *What does the Psalm say to us?*
   After working on the other six questions, the reader, student, and believers-that-we-are must make some effort to relate the Psalm to our own lives.
8. *How can we respond to the Psalm meaningfully?*
   It is not just a matter of offering our own interpretation and application of the Psalm, but it is also important for us to respond to the Psalm in some way that expresses our own faith commitment.

Each of the eight questions will provide the focus for a part of the following process. The process is one that teachers/leaders can engage in preparing to guide a group in its study of a Psalm. Or, the process can be followed by individuals for their own study and personal fulfillment.

I have chosen Psalm 145 as the basis for this activity for several reasons: (1) I responded positively to the Psalm when I read it recently, (2) I had not worked in depth with this Psalm previously, (3) as I reread the Psalm it appeared to have the potential for a fruitful study, and (4) I wanted to work with a Psalm that was not familiar to everyone who might read this book. It is to be expected that some questions (steps in the process) will be more productive than others. This is true of any Psalm.

What Is the Psalm's Type?

As I read Psalm 145 in the *Good News Bible*, I notice immediately that the title used by the translator is "A Hymn of Praise." The footnote adjacent to this title refers to the Hebrew title as "A Song of Praise by David." Already I am confident that this is a Psalm of praise. When I read the first stanza of Psalm 145, the type is confirmed. The words "I will proclaim," "I will thank," or "I will praise" begin each line. The words *praise*, *praised*, *proclaim*, and *thanks* appear seven more times in the Psalm. All of these clues indicate that Psalm 145 is to be considered a Psalm of praise and thanksgiving.

We worked with Psalms of praise and thanksgiving in the previous activity. We identified five different elements that are characteristic of most psalms of this type: (1) introduction, (2) a description of a past distress, (3) a plea for God's help, (4) remembering God's gracious deeds, and (5) an ascription of praise. As I read Psalm 145, I notice that all of the elements are present to some degree but not in the order that they were presented above. The first stanza is the *introduction* in which the Psalmist declares his intent to praise and thank God and to proclaim his greatness.

The *description of a past distress* is only alluded to rather than being spelled out more specifically. The distress is alluded to in words such as: "those who are in trouble," "those who have fallen," and "food when they need it." These clues to the distress of the people are very subtle but nevertheless present.

A *plea for God's help* is also not prominent in Psalm 145. There are just three allusions to those who appeal to God to help them in their distress: "those who call to him" (twice in verse 18) and "he hears their cries" (19).

The element of *remembering God's gracious deeds* is quite evident. There are six references to "acts," "mighty acts," "wonderful deeds," and "mighty deeds"—which all refer to God's acts of creation and salvation. There are other more specific acts of God mentioned: the Lord is "loving and merciful" (8), "faithful to his promises" (13), "helps those who are in trouble" (14), "lifts those who have fallen" (14), "give[s] them food when they need it" (15), "supplies the needs of those who honor him" (19), and "protects everyone who loves him" (20).

The *ascription of praise* is not only in the last verse ("I will always praise the Lord") as it is in many Psalms of this type, but there is also a section, verses 4-7, which describes in a variety of ways that the people will "praise," "proclaim," "speak," "tell," and "sing" about the Lord's gracious deeds. Verses 10-12 again affirm that praise will be offered for who God is and what God has done for the people.

With these few clues about the characteristics of Psalms of praise and thanksgiving and by just reading the text carefully, most of the participants of this activity will be able to determine which type Psalm 145 represents.

What are the Psalm's distinguishing features?

We notice immediately that the RSV title of the Psalm is "A song of praise. Of David." We can skim all of the Psalms or consult a commentary to discover that this is the only one of the one hundred fifty Psalms that is called "a song of praise." "Of David" suggests that David might be the author; however, many biblical scholars attribute this Psalm to a later date, after the return from the Babylonian exile. They suggest that the language of the Psalm has more in common with the development of the Hebrew language at a later time than it does with an earlier time.

If we were to consult a commentary, or a copy of the Jewish translation, we would find out that Psalm 145 is one of the nine acrostic Psalms. Each verse begins with successive letters of the Hebrew alphabet. But, there is a slight problem; there are twenty-two letters in the alphabet and only twenty-one verses in the Psalm. One letter is missing.

Psalm 145 is composed of five stanzas, plus a last verse that serves as a doxology to conclude the Psalm. The poetry style is primarily synonymous parallelism and synthetic parallelism (see chapter 11 for descriptions and examples of each).

One more feature I notice as I read the Psalm again is that there is an erratic mix of the Psalmist addressing God directly and speaking about God. Except for verse 3, the first part of the Psalm (1-13*a*) is addressed *to* God by an individual. Verses 3 and 13*a*-21 are speaking *about* God in the third person.

Where do the cross-references lead?

In Psalm 145 there are no cross-references that make a specific connection between lines of this Psalm with other Psalms or with other passages in the Old and New Testaments. Even though there are no direct cross-references, there are many other Psalms and portions of scripture that contain the same themes—praise of God for the gracious deeds God has done on behalf of the people.

What are the key words and concepts?

We have already dealt with the key words associated with *praise* and *mighty acts*. In reading the Psalm again I do not notice any other individual words that appear frequently in the Psalm. However, I do notice two different categories of words. One category appears primarily in verses 7-9; these are words that describe God's nature. God is described as expressing goodness, kindness, love, mercy, patience (slow to anger), constant love, and compassion. A Bible dictionary or Hebrew lexicon and concordance can give definitions of all these words. This would be a profitable study if group members each worked on a different word. Such a study will reveal that God's grace is truly amazing—it is given freely. The only conditions on which such grace is given are that the people accept it, live righteously, share it with others, and give love to God in return.

The other category of words appears in verses 15 to 20. These are all verbs describing God's acts on behalf of people in need.

God *gives* food to the *hungry*.
God *satisfies* the needs of *all*.
God *supplies* the needs of *those who honor* him.
God *hears* the *cries* of *those who call*.
God *protects everyone* who loves him.
God *destroys* the *wicked*.

We can find many examples where God's people remember specific interventions by God acting for their corporate, as well as individual, welfare.

When you look at the two sets of words, they all add up to an overwhelming affirmation that God is One who is absolutely dependable and faithful. God is to be believed and trusted today and tomorrow because of God's marvelous, past acts of delivering the people.

How is the Psalm presented in other translations?

Comparing several translations usually results in some interesting observations. For this activity I compared four translations: Revised Standard Version (RSV), Jerusalem Bible (JB), *Good News Bible* in Today's English Version (TEV), and the Jewish Translation (JT). In comparing Psalm 145, I discovered:

1. The Jerusalem Bible uses "Yahweh" as the name for God where the other three use "the Lord."
2. In the JT and JB translations, the Hebrew letters are identified—in the JT with the Hebrew characters and in the JB with the name of the letter. With that bit of information, we know immediately that Psalm 145 is an acrostic psalm. Reading the RSV and the TEV translations, we would never have any clue that 145 was an acrostic psalm, especially with only twenty-one verses instead of twenty-two.
3. Both the JB and the RSV translations have a footnote between verses 13 and 14, which is the place where the Hebrew letter "Nun" is missing. The footnote suggests that the line added to verse 13 is found in one ancient Hebrew manuscript. The line reads, "The Lord is faithful in all his words, and gracious in all his deeds" (RSV). The line appears as part of verse 13 in the TEV, but there is no indication that it is a questionable line. The line does not appear at all in the JT.
4. Where the TEV uses words such as *proclaim, thank, praise, speak, tell,* and *sing,* the other three translations for the most part use different words.

TEV	RSV	JT	JB
proclaim	extol	extol	sing
thank	bless	bless	bless
praise	praise	praise	blessing
praised	praised	acclaimed	praising
proclaim	laud	declare	praise
speak	proclaim	talk	proclaim
tell	pour forth	celebrate	celebrate
sing	sing aloud	sing	joyously
		joyously	acclaim

The point of this comparison is to show the wide variety of English words that can be used to translate particular Hebrew words because of the richness of the original language. Even though the TEV consistently uses a more common word in order to facilitate understanding by the ordinary person, there is something missing when the word *tell* is used instead of a word like *celebrate,* which appears in the JT and JB. And *sing* does not quite match *sing joyously.* On the other hand, *thank* in the TEV is more understandable then *bless* used in the other three translations.

5. The Hebrew word *hesed* is translated differently by each translation: "steadfast love" (RSV), "constant love" (TEV), "abounding in kindness" (JT), and "very loving" (JB).

6. It is also enlightening to compare translations at the point of key verses. One example is verses 15 and 16.

The eyes of all look to thee,
   and thou givest them their food in due season.
Thou openest thy hand,
   thou satisfiest the desire of every living thing.
(RSV)

All living things look hopefully to you,
   and you give them food when they need it.
You give them enough
   and satisfy the needs of all.   (TEV)

Patiently all creatures look to you
   to feed them throughout the year;
quick to satisfy every need,
   you feed them all with a generous hand.   (JB)

The eyes of all look to you expectantly,
   and you give them their food when it is due.
You give it openhandedly,
   feeding every creature to it's heart's content. (JT)

Many more comparisons could be made, but these should be sufficient to illustrate the value of having several translations at hand when studying a Psalm. It is not a matter of trying to prove one translation right and the others wrong. Rather it is a way to gain insight and inspiration from the several translations.

How is the Psalm interpreted by others?

In my study I used commentaries by A. A. Anderson, A. B. Rhodes, A. Weiser, and C. Westermann. (Complete information can be found in the bibliography at the end of this book.) Other commentaries can be used. Anderson provides brief specific notes on key words of each verse. From Anderson we learn that "from generation to generation" in verse 4 is a phrase that appears only in this one place in the whole Old Testament. However, the phrase sounds very similar to a line in Psalm 78:6 (TEV) "[teach] so that the next generation might learn them [the laws]." Yes, it is a different Hebrew phrase, but there is a striking similarity in the intent of both phrases; one generation is responsible for sharing with the next generation the good news of God's gracious acts.

Rhodes' notes are brief, too. He does not deal with key words in verses but rather key concepts in stanzas. Rhodes organizes the Psalm around six concepts: God's greatness (1-3), God's mighty acts (4-7), God's compassionate nature (8-9), God's kingdom (10-13*b*), God's faithfulness and grace (13*c*-20), and God's praise (21).

Weiser emphatically suggests that Psalm 145 is a liturgical hymn of the cultic community. He makes this assertion based on the strong emphasis on the kingship of God (vv. 1, 11ff.), praise for the blessing of a rich harvest (vv. 15f.), and the mighty acts of God (vv. 5f.). He concludes that this Psalm was recited at the feast of covenant celebrated in autumn.

Westermann's book is not a commentary as such but is an analysis of Psalms according to two types: laments and praise. He subdivides the two types, thus identifying Psalm 145 and an "imperative Psalm of praise." Its main characteristic is the imperative call to the people to praise God—alternating with descriptions of God's majesty and goodness.

What does the Psalm say to me?

After working with the other six questions, I am better prepared to answer this question than I would be if I just read the Psalm and reflected on it after one reading. That is not to suggest that in order to say what a Psalm means, I must always answer all of the six previous questions. It is possible that an initial reading of a Psalm will uncover much meaning and provide insight.

As I read Psalm 145 I am impressed with how great God is, how marvelous are God's works of

Lord, you have made so many things!
How wisely you made them all!
The earth is filled with your creatures.

Psalm 104:24

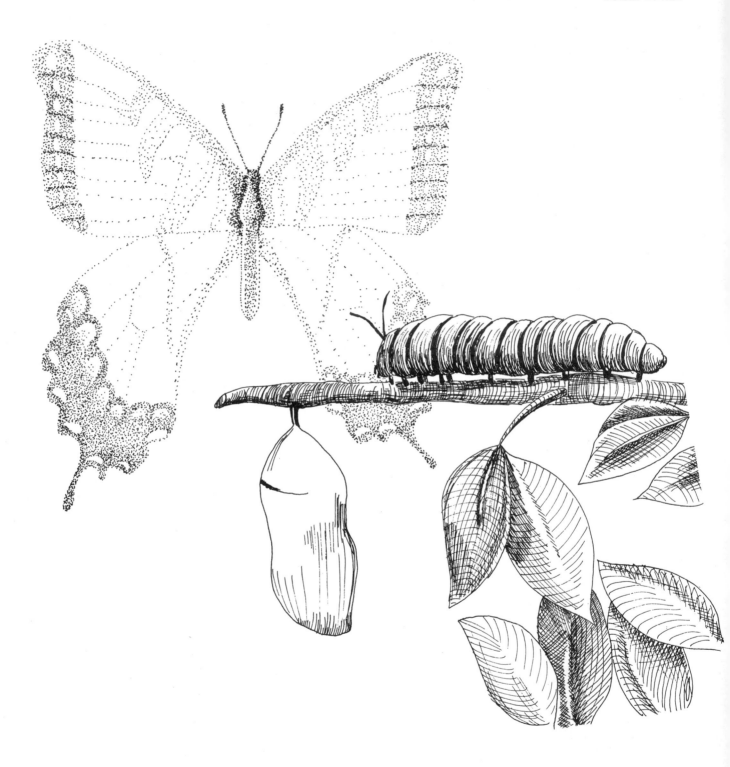

creation and salvation, and how much I, and all humanity, am in need of, dependent upon, and indebted to God. From the perspective of the Christian gospel, I can recite John 3:16 and 2 Corinthians 5:18 with even more conviction. "For God loved the world so much that he gave his only Son, so that everyone who believes in him may not die but have eternal life" (TEV) and "All this is from God, who through Christ reconciled us to himself and gave us the ministry of reconciliation" (RSV). God is truly the one who provides for our needs, hears our cries, saves us, and protects us. God is faithful to all the promises that were made for the liberation and preservation of the specially called people.

Psalm 145, in its several translations, speaks to me of a God who is absolutely dependable. The wars between nations may threaten our security; the unpredictability of the natural elements may distress us; the hostility of neighbors and unreliability of friends may cause us to be angry; and the uncertainty we feel within ourselves may cause us anxiety. However, God is able to deliver us from all these troubles. God has acted throughout all of history for the welfare of those who put their trust in God, and I am very confident God will continue to act in the world where I live for the benefit of all who believe God to be their Creator, Lord, Redeemer, and Protector.

How can I respond to the Psalm meaningfully?

This last question calls for more than a cognitive, well-stated answer. This question calls for a response of the heart as well as the mind. This question asks me to express myself in some creative way that will communicate to God and others what feelings and beliefs have been generated by the study of the Psalm. There are several ways I can respond:

1. I could write my own Psalm of praise and thanksgiving to express my personal response to God for all that has happened for me to believe, to follow, and to serve Jesus Christ as Lord and Savior of my life.

2. If I were capable I could write a song, play a song, or sing a song of praise and thanksgiving. The song could be from the hymnbook. The hymn "O Lord, Thou Art My God and King" is based upon Psalm 145. Or, I could sing a more contemporary song that expresses the praise and thanks I feel.

3. I could also speak to others about my thankfulness toward God for all that has contributed to the preservation and prosperity I have experienced in my life.

4. Another possible way to respond with praise and thanks is through an art form such as taking photos, molding clay, creating with paint, or arranging objects for a collage.

5. Out of my thankfulness I could respond by being of help to someone else who has not experienced the blessings of God as I have. As an individual or with a group I could plan for some way to serve others in the name of God so that they may experience the actions of God that the Psalmist describes in Psalm 145.

In a series of study sessions where time is provided, all the participants can use one of the above options, or others, to respond meaningfully to the word from God they experience in the Psalm.

20

Additional Teaching Activities

Setting the Stage

In each of the nine preceding teaching activities there is sufficient content and process for the teachers/leaders to plan nine to twenty study sessions of one hour or more in length. There are some other activities that I would like to describe that are not as comprehensive as the others. Each of the five activities in this chapter is presented briefly, with no attempt made to provide all of the content and process necessary for a full treatment of the topic. However, teachers/leaders may adapt these activities to include them as part of other sessions, or combine two of them for one complete session. Also, the activities may be expanded so that what is suggested here can serve as the basis for a complete session.

ONE: Psalm 119

Psalm 119 is the longest Psalm, with one hundred seventy-six verses. As mentioned in chapter 11, this Psalm is one of the nine acrostic Psalms. It is also the most complex of the acrostic Psalms. We recall that there are twenty-two letters in the Hebrew alphabet. In Psalm 119 there are twenty-two stanzas of eight verses each. Not only does each stanza begin with the appropriate letter of the Hebrew alphabet, but each of the eight verses of the stanza also begins with the same letter. Try sometime to compose eight lines or eight verses beginning each with the same letter, and then imagine how difficult it would be to do that for each letter of the alphabet. To get a sense of what I am describing, I tried to write eight lines beginning with the letter "a."

All of us as your people, O God,
  ask for your forgiveness of our sin.
Alone we are powerless to save ourselves,
  as we recognize our need for deliverance.
Amazing is your grace that reaches out to us

Almighty God, our Lord and Redeemer.
Above all, O God, we are most grateful;
  Accept our praise and thanks for your grace.

Part of this activity can involve the participants, each with one or two different letters of the alphabet, in attempting to compose eight-line stanzas like the one above. Such attempts will help the participants appreciate the fantastic literary achievement that Psalm 119 represents.

Another interesting feature of Psalm 119 is that there is a different word in each verse in each stanza that is a synonym of the word *law*. In some verses there are two synonyms. This is repeated in each of the twenty-two stanzas of the Psalm. We can understand why the Psalm has been called a hymn in praise of the law.

When I compared four translations (RSV, TEV, JB, and JT), I discovered that in only two instances did all four use the same word: *commandments* and *ways*. In all other instances there were from two to four different English words used to translate the same Hebrew word. Among the four translations, all of the additional following synonyms for *law* were used: testimonies, statutes, precepts, ordinances, judgments, teachings, instructions, decrees, rules, word, promise, paths, and wondrous acts. Given additional translations you might find even more synonyms.

In addition to participants trying their hand at writing eight-line acrostic Psalms, they can each work on one or more stanzas to seek answers to four questions. (It is best if all twenty-two stanzas are divided up among the group members.)
1. What synonyms for law are present in the stanzas?
2. What are the promised rewards for devotion to the law?
3. What are the threatened punishments for disobeying the law?
4. What are some of the Psalmist's expressions of high regard for the law?

After sharing answers to these questions and discussing Psalm 119 as a whole, it might be enlightening to read some New Testament passages dealing with the law—such as Romans 2:1-29 and 7:7-25—to see how these approaches to the law compare with the Psalmist's approach.

TWO: God's Favor Is toward . . .

One approach to Bible study, and to the Psalms, is to focus on a particular theme and to explore the scriptures to gather resources in order to make some statements about the theme. Biblical theology is a result of this approach where biblical scholars explore themes such as the doctrine of God, the doctrine of salvation, the covenant relationships between God and the human person, the doctrine of revelation, and others. In one sense when we focus on a particular psalm type, we are also focusing on a theme such a lament, praise, trust, etc. However, there are other themes that are appropriate to Psalms. Some potential themes are: the nature of God, the nature of the human person, the nature of life and death, the concept of righteousness, the concepts of war and peace, as well as many others.

There is a way to work with a group to develop an overview of Psalms regarding a particular theme. It works best if there are fifteen or more persons in a group. Assign each individual an equal number of Psalms by dividing the one hundred fifty Psalms among the members of the group. The task of each person is to read or skim the assigned Psalms, looking for passages relevant to the designated theme. After everyone has had time to gather evidence, there should be sufficient time for sharing their findings. When all the data is shared, then teachers/leaders can guide a discussion that will help analyze and interpret the information.

As an example of a theme, look in Psalms to see to whom God's favor is directed. Many who take a social action or liberation theology approach to the Christian faith use the writings of the prophets, gospels, and epistles as a basis for their convictions. Psalms are not ordinarily used as a primary resource for understanding that God's favor is toward the weak, the poor, the homeless, the prisoners, and others experiencing distress. In one conference I led, I decided to involve the group in searching all of Psalms to find whatever evidence there is to show how God's favor is directed. We divided Psalms among all of us and looked for two things that we listed in two columns with the headings:

1) God's favor is toward . . .
2) God's favor is expressed as . . .

We found at least eighty references in approximately fifty Psalms in a rather quick skimming of Psalms. Before doing the skimming, we all looked at Psalm 146:7-9, which provided a good example of what we were looking for.

Verse	God's favor is toward . . .	God's favor is expressed as . . .
7	the oppressed	judgment in their favor
7	the hungry	provision of food
8	prisoners	being set free
8	the blind	being given sight
8	those who have fallen	being lifted up
8	the righteous people	being loved by God
9	strangers	protection

With this example clearly in mind, the participants were able to find many references. After gathering all the data and then reflecting on it, the participants became aware that God's favor is directed to all who are oppressed, who are in physical or spiritual need, or who experience some personal distress. God's favor is also directed toward the righteous, those who love God and who obey his commandments, and those who are faithful to the covenant relationship with God.

In one group of educators and lay Bible study leaders, a wealthy person made the observation, "If you are not poor, hungry, a widow, or orphan, or oppressed in any way, then you better be righteous." Then we discussed what it means to be righteous and one of the conclusions was that to be righteous is to love God with your whole being and to love those whom God loves. In other words, we as God's people are called upon to respond to the needs of the hungry, the strangers, the distressed, the helpless, and all who are oppressed in one way or another. As a result of this study, the whole group realized that

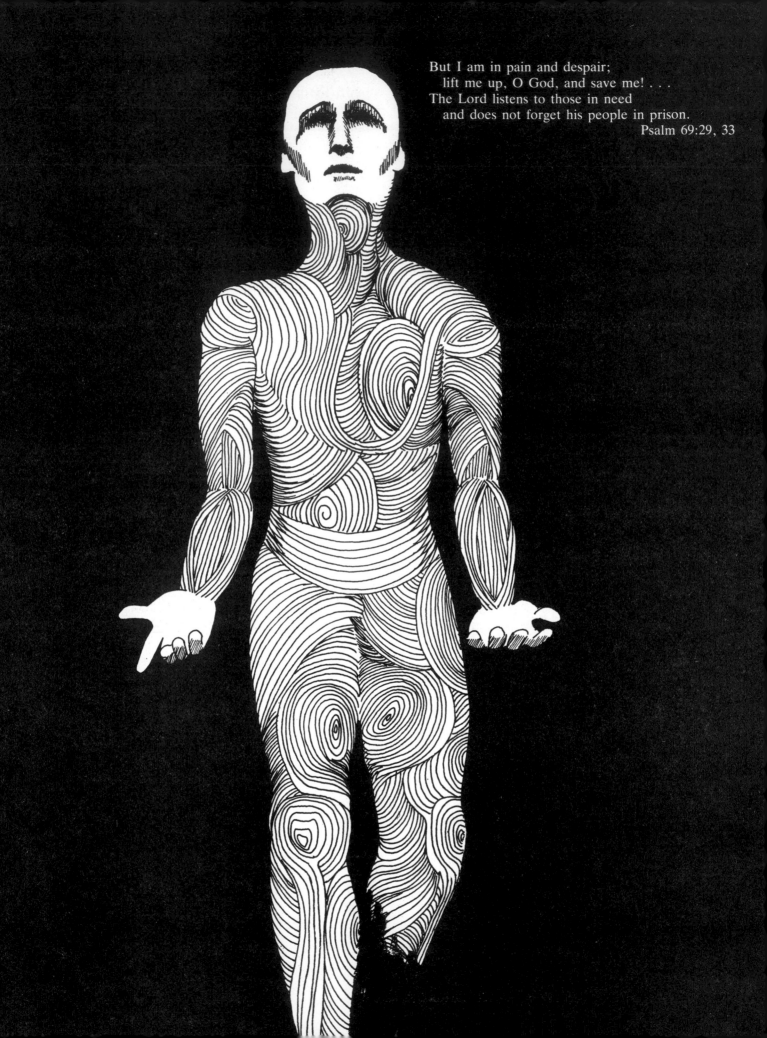

But I am in pain and despair;
   lift me up, O God, and save me! . . .
The Lord listens to those in need
   and does not forget his people in prison.
                Psalm 69:29, 33

Psalms, as well as the prophets and the gospels, call us to minister actively on behalf of those in need.

THREE: Psalms in the New Testament

In the Gospels there are at least forty-three cross-references to Psalms. There are many other cross-references to Psalms in the other books of the New Testament. There are twenty-one Psalms references in the Gospel of Matthew alone. It is important for students of the Bible to see the Old and New Testaments as two parts of one whole story. One way to get this picture is to do some intentional work of comparing the Psalms passages with the way they are used in the books of the New Testament. There are two ways to go about this:

1. Assign small groups of participants to specific books of the New Testament, divide the chapters of the book among the members of the group, and look for Psalm cross-references. As persons find cross-references, they are to read both the New Testament passage (more than one verse in order to get a sense of the context in which the verse appears) and the Psalm passage. Then they should answer three questions:
   a. What type of Psalm is used?
   b. Is the type consistent with the context in which it is quoted?
   c. What contribution does the Psalm passage make to the New Testament passage?
2. Another way to organize the activity is to assign members of the group a number of Psalms, letting them survey the cross-references to see where there are New Testament passages that are noted. Again, the same three questions can be used to guide the process.

During the season of Lent, a profitable study can be developed around the penitential Psalms that have references in the passion narratives of the gospels. Small groups could work on each of Psalms 22, 31, 41, and 69. Participants can be directed to read the Psalm from the perspective of Jesus' experiences between his entry into Jerusalem and his crucifixion. Two questions are appropriate for reflection and discussion:

1. How does the Psalm help us understand the passion of Jesus?
2. How does the passion of Jesus as recorded in the Gospel help us understand the Psalm?

Another way to work with Psalms and the New Testament is to consider passages in both where a common theme is expressed or possibly a contrasting concept is evident when two passages are juxtaposed. There are many examples of Psalms verses that are not quoted directly in the New Testament, but the theme of these Psalms verses is clearly present in the New Testament (see examples below). By comparing passages like these we not only increase our understanding of the concept, but we can see in another way the continuity between the two Testaments. Members of a study group can easily discover passages where there is linkage between Psalms and New Testament passages. It is important for each participant to have access to a concise Bible concordance so that they can find passages they are looking for more easily. The following directions can guide a group's exploration:

1. Start either with a familiar Psalm or with a familiar New Testament passage. Identify what you think is the central meaning of the passage.
2. Using a concordance to focus on key words, try to find a passage in the other portion of scripture that expresses a similar meaning, features the same concept, or offers a contrasting point of view.
3. If you have difficulty locating a passage, perhaps others in the group can help.
4. Be ready to share your findings.

For some brief examples of passages that were linked together by one study group, see page 106.

FOUR: Psalms in the Lectionary

Many Christian chuches are now using a common lectionary that provides selected Bible readings from Old Testament, Gospel, Epistle, and Psalms for each Sunday and other special days and seasons of the church year. There are three annual cycles of texts so that after three years, most of the major texts of scripture will

1. Psalm 23:1	The Lord is my shepherd, I have everything I need.	
John 10:11	[Jesus said,] "I am the good shepherd, who is willing to die for the sheep."	
2. Psalm 119:105	Your word is a lamp to guide me and a light for my path.	
John 8:12	[Jesus said,] "I am the light of the world. Whoever follows me will have the light of life and will never walk in darkness."	

3. Psalm 49:7-9	A person can never redeem himself;
	    he cannot pay God the price for his life,
	    because the payment for a human life
	        is too great.
	What he could pay would never be enough
	    to keep him from the grave,
	    to let him live forever.	

Romans 5:7	It is a difficult thing for someone to die for a righteous person . . . But God has shown us how much he loves us—it was while we were still sinners that Christ died for us! By his sacrificial death we are now put right with God. . . .	

have been covered. In churches where the lectionary texts are the readings for each Sunday and the pastor bases the sermon on one or more of the texts, the congregation is exposed to and nurtured by the whole of the Bible.

In reviewing the combinations of passages for many of the Sundays, I have noticed that the Psalm text is more often than not selected to coordinate with the theme of the other texts. I made a chart to see which Psalms were included in the lectionary and how often they were used. It is interesting to me that only eighty-four of the one hundred fifty Psalms were used. Twenty-six of those eighty-four Psalms were used three or more times. Psalm 118 was included eight times, more often than any other Psalm. I looked to see which Psalms were omitted from the lectionary to see if there was any pattern. I discovered that only a few of the lament Psalms were used, even though over one-third of the Psalms are laments. The laments that are included are primarily those that are associated with the season of Lent and Holy Week, which we have identified as penitential Psalms in a previous activity. Only two of the six Zion Psalms and two of the eight royal Psalms are included in the lectionary. As I expected, most of the praise and thanksgiving Psalms and Psalms of trust were used. The exclusion of Psalm 136 surprises me very much. It seems to me that Psalm 136 should have been included because its very structure—a litany—makes it quite appropriate for liturgical use.

Working at seeing the linkage between the Psalm text and the other passages for a given Sunday is a task very similar to the previous activity where participants tried to make their own connections between Psalms and the New Testament. That activity can be used either before or after this activity with the lectionary.

In a church where the use of the lectionary is a regular part of the worship experience, it would be appropriate and helpful for a study group to spend some time engaging in this activity. Some directions might be:

Directions

1. Work in small groups of two or three
2. Each group work with one of the following sets of texts.

First Sunday of Advent

Isaiah 2:1-5
Psalm 122
Romans 13:8-14
Matthew 24:27-44

First Sunday after Epiphany

Isaiah 42:1-9
Psalm 89
Acts 10:34-38
Matthew 3:13-17

Ash Wednesday

Joel 2:1-2, 12-17
Psalm 103
2 Corinthians 5:20b-6:10
Matthew 6:1-6, 16-21

First Sunday in Lent

Genesis 2:4b-9, 15-17, 25-3:7
Psalm 51
Romans 5:12-19
Matthew 4:1-11

Palm Sunday

Isaiah 42:21-25
Psalm 22:1-21
Philippians 2:5-11
Matthew 26:36-75, 27:1-54

Easter Sunday

Exodus 14:1-14, 21-25, 15:20-21
Psalm 118:14-29
Colossians 3:1-4
John 20:1-10

Pentecost Sunday

Ezekiel 11:17-20
Psalm 104
Acts 2:1-11
John 20:19-23

Last Sunday of Church Year

Ezekiel 34:11-17
Psalm 95:1-7
I Corinthians 15:20-28
Matthew 25:31-46

3. Read all four texts.

4. Reflect on and discuss these five questions:
   a. What is the common theme present in all four texts?

   b. Does any one text seem not to fit? Why?

   c. How do you think the Psalm text fits with the others?

   d. Is there any other Psalm text that you would select in preference to the one listed?

   e. If you were to summarize the four texts in your words, what would the message be?

5. Prepare to share your observations and your message with others.

FIVE: Psalms in the Hymnal

In almost every hymnal there is an index in the back that lists all of the hymns that are either based upon specific biblical texts or where the theme of the hymn or stanzas of the hymn matches the theme of a biblical text. Pastors use this index when planning an order of service so that the hymns sung by the congregation will relate to the scripture passages and the sermon. In addition, there are two very helpful books that not only list all the texts of the lectionary for three years but also list a number of recommended hymns for each Sunday. The two books are: *A Handbook for the Lectionary* by Horace T. Allen and *The Prayer Book Guide to Christian Education* by the Episcopal Church Center (see bibliography for more details).

I have suggested in several of the praying and teaching activities that it would be appropriate to include a hymn as part of the session. For many of the other sessions, if not all of them, it would be equally appropriate to sing a hymn or two at the beginning, during, or at the end of the session. When you look at the index of scriptural allusions in hymns, the list for Psalms is as much as five times longer than the list for any other book of the Bible. Of course, Psalms is a longer book than any other; however, Psalms is also the richest, most poetic, and most devotional of all the books of the Bible.

There are several brief activities that can involve members of a group in exploring the church's hymnals, as well as the Psalms.

1. Invite persons to look at their favorite hymns to see if any can find their origin in the Psalms. If so, read the Psalm as well as the hymn to see how each enhances the other.

2. A similar process can begin with persons looking at favorite Psalms and then checking the index in the hymnal to see if any of those Psalms have one or more hymns that express the message of the Psalm. Again, read the hymn as well as the Psalm.

3. A group can start with a psalm type such as praise and thanksgiving, trust, creation, or lament and check to see how many of the psalms of that type have corresponding hymns.

4. Of course, an activity that must be included is a hymn sing where time is provided for the singing of a number of hymns that are related to Psalms. The hymns can be favorite hymns with a Psalm base or unfamiliar hymns that are selected because of their Psalm reference. Or, hymns expressing one type of psalm can be sung in one session.

Bibliography

Translations of the Psalms

The Book of Psalms: A New Translation According to the Traditional Hebrew Text. Philadelphia: Jewish Publication Society of America, 1972.

Good News Bible: The Bible in Today's English Version. New York: American Bible Society, 1976. This translation includes a word list, index of names and places, and Annie Vallotton's line drawings and interpretative headings for each of the Psalms.

The Jerusalem Bible. New York: Doubleday & Co., 1966.

The New English Bible. Oxford Study Edition. New York: Oxford University Press, 1976. The study notes for each Psalm are brief and helpful. Each Psalm is identified by type.

New International Version. Grand Rapids: Zondervan, 1978.

Revised Standard Version. New York: American Bible Society, 1973.

Commentaries on Psalms

Anderson, A. A. *New Century Bible Commentary: The Book of Psalms,* 2 vols. Grand Rapids: William B. Eerdmans Publishing Co., 1972.

Buttrick, George Arthur, ed. *The Interpreter's Bible: Psalms and Proverbs,* Vol. 4. Nashville: Abingdon Press, 1955.

Dahood, Mitchell, ed. Anchor Bible Series. Vols. 16, 17 and 17A. New York: Doubleday & Co., 1965.

Knight, George A. F. *The Daily Study Bible Series: Psalms.* 2 vols. Philadelphia: Westminster Press, 1982.

Murphy, Roland E. *Proclamation Commentaries: The Psalms, Job.* Philadelphia: Fortress Press, 1977.

Rhodes, Arnold B. *The Layman's Bible Commentary: The Book of Psalms.* Vol. 9. Atlanta: John Knox Press, 1960.

Weiser, Arthur. *The Psalms: A Commentary.* Philadelphia: Westminster Press, 1962.

Interpretations of Psalms

Anderson, Bernard W. *Out of the Depths: The Psalms Speak for Us Today.* Philadelphia: Westminster Press, 1970.

Barclay, William. *The Lord is My Shepherd: Expositions of Selected Psalms.* Philadelphia: Westminster Press, 1980.

Botz, Paschal. *Runways to God: The Psalms as Prayer.* Collegeville, Minn.: Liturgical Press, 1979.

Lewis, C. S. *Reflections on the Psalms.* New York: Harcourt, Brace & Co., 1958.

Routley, Erik. *Exploring the Psalms.* Philadelphia: Westminster Press, 1975.

Westermann, Claus. *Praise and Lament in the Psalms.* Atlanta: John Knox Press, 1981.

_____, *The Psalms: Structure, Content and Message.* Minneapolis: Augsburg Publishing House, 1980.

Devotional Books Featuring Psalms

Bonhoeffer, Dietrich. *Psalms: The Prayerbook of the Bible.* Minneapolis: Augsburg Publishing House, 1970.

Brandt, Leslie F. *Psalms/Now* St. Louis: Concordia Publishing House, 1973.

Brueggemann, Walter. *Praying the Psalms.* Winona, Minn.: Saint Mary's Press, 1982.

Dunlop, Laurence. *Patterns of Prayer in the Psalms.* New York: Seabury Press, 1982.

Merton, Thomas. *Praying the Psalms.* Collegeville, Minn.: Liturgical Press, 1956.

Old, Hughes Oliphant. *Praying with the Bible.* Philadelphia: Geneva Press, 1980.

Troeger, Thomas H. *Rage! Reflect, Rejoice! Praying with the Psalmist.* Philadelphia: Westminster Press, 1977.

Lectionaries and Worship Aids

Allen, Horace T., Jr. *A Handbook for the Lectionary.* Philadelphia: Geneva Press, 1980.

Hessel, Dieter T., ed. *Social Themes of the Christian Year: A Commentary on the Lectionary.* Philadelphia: Geneva Press, 1983.

The Prayer Book Guide to Christian Education. New York: Seabury Press, 1983.

Shepherd, Massey H., Jr. *A Liturgical Psalter for the Christian Year.* Minneapolis: Augsburg Publishing House, 1976.

_____, *The Psalms in Christian Worship: A Practical Guide.* Collegeville, Minn.: Liturgical Press, 1976.

Audio-Visual Resources

I have not been able to locate many audio-visual resources that feature the Psalms. The following three resources are all well done and will be helpful to any teachers/leaders who choose to use them.

Psalms—A series of four cassette tapes that present all one hundred fifty Psalms in the Today's English Version. (Also available in Revised Standard and King James Versions.)Produced by and available from the American Bible Society, 1865 Broadway, New York, NY 10023.

Psalm Prayers—A series of five filmstrips and cassette tapes featuring interpretations of five Psalms: 31, 32, 103, 121, and 138. Produced by Gerard A. Pottebaum and available from: Treehaus Communications, Inc., P. O. Box 249, Loveland, OH 45140.

Worship and the Arts—A series of six kits on worship, music, dance, and the arts. One kit features Psalm 150 and includes a filmstrip and cassette, with music by Doc Severinsen. Produced by and available from: The Joint Office of Worship, Presbyterian Church (USA), 1044 Alta Vista Road, Louisville, KY 40205.

Appendix: Classification of Psalms by Type

Psalms of Praise and Thanksgiving
  9, 29, 30, 33, 40:1-11, 65, 66, 67, 92, 95, 100, 103, 107, 111, 113, 116, 117, 124, 133, 134, 138, 145, 147, 149, and 150.
Creation Psalms
  8, 19:1-6, 104, and 148
Salvation History Psalms
  78, 105, 106, 135, and 136
Psalms Proclaiming the Lord as King
  47, 68, 89, 93, 96, 97, and 99
Hymns of Zion (Praise of Jerusalem)
  46, 48, 76, 87, 132, and 144
Royal Psalms (Featuring the King of Israel)
  2, 18, 20, 21, 45, 72, 101, and 110
Individual Psalms of Lament
  3, 5, 6, 7, 10, 13, 17, 23, 25, 28, 35, 38, 39, 41, 42, 43,

51, 54, 55, 56, 57, 59, 61, 64, 69, 70, 71, 86, 88, 102, 109, 120, 130, 139, 140, 141, 142, and 143
Community Psalms of Lament
  12, 44, 58, 60, 74, 79, 80, 83, 85, 89, 90, 94, 129, and 137
Psalms of Trust
  4, 11, 16, 23, 26, 27, 31, 62, 63, 91, 121, 125, 131, and 146
Torah Psalms
  19:7-14 and 119
Wisdom Psalms
  1, 34, 36, 37, 49, 73, 112, 127, and 128
Liturgical Psalms
  15, 24, 81, 84, 115, 118, 122, and 136
Psalms of Mixed Types (Difficult to Classify)
  14, 32, 50, 52, 53, 75, 82, 108, 114, 123, and 126

Index of Psalms

The following references are places where the Psalm is either quoted in the text of this book or it is included as part of a praying or teaching activity.